Dear Liz:

HOLY LIVING

Hope this sters your
heart as it has mine; we
have such a wonderful God
"who only doeth wondrous things"

Ps. 72:18

Love in Him,

Dorothy.

GOD'S PROVISION FOR

HOLY LIVING

WILLIAM CULBERTSON
President of Moody Bible Institute

Foreword by
A. T. HOUGHTON
Chairman, Keswick Convention Council

MOODY PRESS
CHICAGO

First published 1957

Moody Book Edition 1970

CONTENTS

FOREWORD

THESE PAGES contain the Bible readings delivered by Dr. William Culbertson in the big
tent at the Keswick Convention in England in
July 1957. For anyone who was privileged to
hear the author as morning by morning he unfolded his theme of God's Provision for Holy
Living, it may be possible to recapture the into-
nation of his voice as with the deepest sincerity
and as man to man he gripped his audience with
the proclamation of the glorious inheritance of
the people of God.

The book needs to be read with this in mind,
for the reader will find no polished literary pro-
duction and well-turned sentences which delight
the ear, but as he reads he may well find that the
speaker's message goes straight to the heart, and
the blessing which came to that vast audience of
some thousands of people will be multiplied in
the hearts of a much larger unseen audience
which reads only the printed page.

In his treatment of the gracious provision of Father, Son and Holy Spirit, leading up to being "filled with all the fulness of God," Dr. Culbertson is in the true Keswick tradition, and this Foreword may suitably conclude with two quotations which may whet the appetite of the reader to study the whole book:

Why talk of a life of victory if sinless perfection is not possible? The answer is simple. Far more of victory can be experienced by any child of God than he has yet experienced. It is apparent from God's Word that God wants us to live holy lives. More than that, He has provided for us to do so.

If God would give us even a handful of people who really mean business with Him, who would go all out for the Lord, who would in utter surrender and absolute faith walk with the Lord, the ends of the earth would feel the impact of that kind of living. We need Christians full of the Holy Ghost.

A. T. HOUGHTON

All Scripture quotations are taken from the American Standard Version (1901).

1

BASIC CONSIDERATIONS

Most Christians desire more likeness to Christ than they have experienced. That fact in itself is not to be disparaged. We can truly thank God if there is discontent with present attainments and a holy aspiration for more complete realization of the life that triumphs. However, many of us become greatly discouraged because the tenor of our lives seems to be one of defeat rather than triumph. Is there even one of us who deep in his heart believes that either Holy Scripture or propriety support the idea that a Christian must always be in the doldrums of defeat—always failing? Is there not that which Dr. Charles Gallaudet Trumbull used to call "the life that wins"?

"Be careful," says the advocate of old-line conservatism, "you will be guilty of teaching the doctrine of sinless perfection." We heartily deny any such allegation. As a matter of fact, we have been too well taught as to the biblical doctrine of sin to be caught in that error. We stand absolutely on the divine dictum that the human heart is deceitful above all things and is desperately wicked. We agree that even the saint must say, if he speaks truthfully, "In me, that is, in my flesh, dwelleth no good thing" (Rom. 7:18). For a Christian to say he has no sin is to be self-deceived (I John 1:8), and to say he has not sinned is to make God a liar (I John 1:10). Never make your definition of sin so narrow that you dare claim sinlessness. The standard of the Bible is the glory of God (Rom. 3:23). Anything short of that norm is sin—even though we call our actions merely mistakes.

But why talk of a life of victory if sinless perfection is not possible? The answer is simple. Far more of victory can be experienced by any child of God than he has yet experienced. It is apparent from God's Word that God wants us to live holy lives. More than that, He has provided for us to do so. It is because so many of God's dear people are ignorant of these provisions that I am emboldened to write. I do not claim originality. Others have been taught of God, and by God's grace I have entered in.

Perhaps one other word should be said before we proceed with our subject. The life that wins is not quietism as it is usually defined by theologians. Victory is not found in a passivity that lets another—even God—do everything. There is a fight of faith. There is a battle, a conflict. No one knows that fact better than the one who begins to enter into the fullness of the life God has for him.

Surrender is not passivity; it is the definite, deliberate, volitional act of the regenerated Christian wittingly giving the Lord Jesus Christ the place of lordship. As a matter of fact, that lordship becomes meaningful, not by passivity, but by diligent study of the Word of God, by earnest, importunate prayer, by the exercise of wholehearted, firm faith, and by absolute, unquestioned obedience. That there is divine help for that man ought to be acknowledged by all who know God. And, to take the next step, let it be understood that that help is the Lord Himself— for He is our victory.

What we are talking about, therefore, is a life, hereinafter described in biblical terms, which is possible only to that person who has been born again by the Holy Spirit and who has entered into the practical as well as the positional sanctifying work of the same Holy Spirit.

Does the Bible present such a life? Indeed it does. Think of these scriptures:

I came that they may have life, and may have it abundantly (John 10:10).

For if, by the trespass of the one, death reigned through the one; much more shall they that receive the abundance of grace and of the gift of righteousness reign in life through the one, even Jesus Christ (Rom. 5:17).

But thanks be unto God, who always leadeth us in triumph in Christ (II Cor. 2:14).

His divine power hath granted unto us all things that pertain unto life and godliness, through the knowledge of him that called us by his own glory and virtue (II Peter 1:3).

Life abundant, reigning in life, triumph, all things that pertain to life and godliness—what do we know of them in experience?

"But," you ask, "if I am a Christian, does that not mean that my standing is perfect before God?" Indeed it does. Listen:

. . . holy brethren (Heb. 3:1).

And such [read verse 10] were some of you: but ye were washed, but ye were sanctified, but ye were justified in the name of the Lord Jesus Christ (I Cor. 6:11).

By which will we have been sanctified through the offering of the body of Jesus Christ once for all (Heb. 10:10).

For by one offering he hath perfected for ever them that are sanctified (Heb. 10:14).

14

. . . Christ Jesus, who was made unto us . . .
righteousness and sanctification . . . (I Cor.
1:30).

What a grand and glorious fact! Forensically,
judicially, positionally, as to standing—made perfect!

But what about our practice, our state? Ah,
there's the rub. Nevertheless, it is true, "his divine power hath granted unto us all things that
pertain unto life and godliness" (II Peter 1:3).

It is God's provisions for our entering into
such a life that we want to look into with you.
The desire which should be ours was expressed
by the apostle Paul.

I press on, if so be that I may lay hold on
that for which also I was laid hold on by Christ
Jesus. Brethren, I count not myself yet to have
laid hold: but . . . I press on toward the goal
unto the prize of the high calling of God in
Christ Jesus (Phil. 3:12-14).

Mark it well, the apostle did not say he had at-
tained. Let not one of us say so either. The
scriptural advice is good: "Let another man
praise thee, and not thine own mouth" (Prov.
27:2). Christlike character may be seen; when
you claim it, it has long since disappeared.

15

2

THE CALL TO HOLINESS

THOUGH MEN, even good men, have seemingly done their best to discredit the Bible word *holiness,* nevertheless it should not be forgotten. Dismissed by some, unscripturally exaggerated by others, it is nonetheless a most important word. I am not much for figures, but somewhere I read that the word *holy* and its cognates (*holiness, sanctify, sanctification*) occur 841 times in the Bible. Evidently it has some importance!

In the Bible, holiness is always rooted in the character of God (Lev. 11:44-45; 19:2; 20:7-8; I Peter 1:15-16). It is therefore advisable to see something of the way in which the holiness of God is described in His Word. However much Eliphaz may have missed the mark in his accusation of Job as a sinner, he had some keen insights into the character and ways of God, though even here he must be checked (cf. Job 42:7). He said of God: "Shall a man be more pure than his

Maker? Behold, he putteth no trust in his servants; and his angels he chargeth with folly" (Job 4:17-18). And again, "Yea, the heavens are not clean in his sight" (Job 15:15).

Though Bildad was far less taught than Eliphaz, who is to say that he was wrong when he uttered a similar word: "Behold, even the moon hath no brightness, and the stars are not pure in his sight" (Job 25:5). It was Moses who sang of God as "glorious in holiness" (Exodus 15:11).

But we can perhaps best understand the overwhelming sense of His holiness by the response of four great and good men when they had a vision of our great God.

Job said: "I have heard of thee by the hearing of the ear; but now mine eye seeth thee: wherefore I abhor myself, and repent in dust and ashes" (Job 42:5-6).

Isaiah said: "Woe is me! for I am undone; because I am a man of unclean lips, and I dwell in the midst of a people of unclean lips: for mine eyes have seen the King, Jehovah of hosts" (Isa. 6:5).

Daniel said: "My comeliness was turned in me into corruption, and I retained no strength" (Dan. 10:8).

John said: "And when I saw him, I fell at his feet as one dead" (Rev. 1:17).

17

Is it any marvel that the seraphim continually cry, "Holy, holy, holy, is Jehovah of hosts: the whole earth is full of his glory" (Isa. 6:3)?

But what is the command of this thrice-holy God? Carefully ponder these words of Scripture:

> For I am Jehovah your God: sanctify yourselves therefore, and be ye holy; for I am holy . . . ye shall therefore be holy, for I am holy (Lev. 11:44-45).

> Ye shall be holy; for I Jehovah your God am holy (Lev. 19:2).

> Sanctify yourselves therefore, and be ye holy; for I am Jehovah your God. And ye shall keep my statutes, and do them: I am Jehovah who sanctifieth you (Lev. 20:7-8).

> Like as he who called you is holy, be ye yourselves also holy in all manner of living; because it is written, Ye shall be holy; for I am holy (I Peter 1:15-16).

> Ye therefore shall be perfect, as your heavenly Father is perfect (Matt. 5:48).

Alas, how can we be holy? The standard is too high, it is utterly beyond us. Is that your response? If it is, it is good. Let us admit at once, *we* cannot live that kind of life. Captain Reginald Wallis used to say that the greatest thing he learned after becoming a Christian was that he could not live the Christian life. If this life is lived, it will be the result of supernatural power. In essence, Christianity is supernatural. The Christian life is essentially miraculous—in its commencement, in its continuation, and in its consummation.

The real question, therefore, is twofold: What are the provisions that God has made for living such a life, and How do I make them mine? Surely, we do not question that God has made provision. It is unthinkable that God would ask us to be anything or do anything without providing us with the power to be and to do.

Now the first answer I want to give to these questions is so simple, so apparent, that it would hardly seem necessary to mention it. Yet I want to be as helpful as I can, and I want to address myself to the most uninformed and youngest Christian. So let me recite what is perfectly obvious to most Christians.

Those of us who use the Liturgy are used to praying a sentence in what is called *A General Thanksgiving*: "We bless Thee for our creation, preservation, and all the blessings of this life; but above all, for Thine inestimable love in the redemption of the world by our Lord Jesus Christ; for the means of grace, and for the hope of glory." It is indeed the right thing, the proper

19

thing, to thank our God for all these blessings—and among them are "the means of grace."

What are these means of grace? How is grace communicated to us? What are the well-known means which God has put at our disposal that we who are Christians may grow in grace and in the knowledge of our Lord and Saviour Jesus Christ?

Your intelligence forbids that I should do more than mention them. Nevertheless, they are important, and they are truly wonderful provisions of our loving Lord. Among them are (1) the reading of the Word of God; (2) the privilege of prayer; (3) the fellowship of the saints (particularly in the local church); (4) the preaching and teaching of the Word of God by Spirit-taught and Spirit-gifted men; (5) the sacraments —the ordinances of baptism and holy communion; (6) the opportunity for Christian witness.

Though well known, these matters are tremendously important. Perhaps there are those of us who would profit greatly by a full rehearsal of the meaning and the necessity of these elementary considerations, which somehow or other have become meaningless in experience, if not in theory. In any case, may I affirm most emphatically that it is my conviction that no Christian can be strong, or what God desires him to be, if he neglects the means of grace.

The application of these provisions is simple enough. With all the power of your renewed mind in Christ Jesus, take yourself by the scruff of the neck, if necessary, and make time to read the Word, to pray, to go to church, to participate in the ministry of the church, to witness for Christ. No Christian who is yielded to God and who trusts God, can use the means of grace without finding grace to grow in grace.

However, important as this provision for holy living is, with God's help I want to proceed to provisions (including a fuller comment concerning the Word of God) which may not be so well known by the rank and file of Christians.

Each Person of the holy, adorable Trinity—three Persons, one God—is presented in the Word of God as having intimate connection with the sanctification of God's children. Our heavenly Father has given us His Word and grants us His fatherly care and training—both for our holiness. The blessed and only Son of the Father, the Lord Jesus Christ, through His cross, our union with Him, His present ministry and His return, provides for our living for Him. The Comforter, the Holy Spirit of God, the Sanctifier of the faithful, has provided for our holiness by His work of regeneration **as well as by the** fact of His indwelling. Here then are at least eight divine provisions: (1) the Word of God, (2) the chastisement of the Father, (3) the cross of Christ, (4) our union with Christ, (5) our Lord's present ministry, (6) the return of our Lord, (7) the creation of the new man, (8) the indwelling of the Holy Spirit.

3

THE HEAVENLY FATHER'S LOVING PROVISION: THE WORD OF GOD

NOT FOR ONE MOMENT do we minimize the importance of the Word of God as the enlightener of men, the instrument used by the Holy Spirit in regeneration, the revealer of the will and way of God for His children, and the discloser of the prophetic events yet to take place. But having said all that, there is yet more. The Word of God itself is that which, given by the heavenly Father, when believed and hidden in the heart by God's children, has power to help the child of God to victory. In other words, there is a sanctifying power in the blessed Word of God when it is in a believing heart.

How thankful we should be that God has indeed spoken. "God, having of old time spoken unto the fathers in the prophets by divers portions and in divers manners, hath at the end of these days spoken unto us in his Son" (Heb. 1: 1-2). This blessed revelation which we have from God in the Old and New Testaments of our canonical Scriptures is a treasure indeed.

Long ago many of us learned a verse of Scripture which bears hard on the subject before us: "Thy word have I laid up in my heart, that I might not sin against thee" (Ps. 119:11). Of course we recognize that it is the Word of God which is the touchstone to show to us definitely what is right and what is wrong. In this sense the Word of God in our hearts directs our paths so that we do not sin against Him.

But surely beyond the mere pointing out of the path of rectitude, as great and wonderful a blessing as that is, is the additional fact that the Word of God has great power in itself. Used effectively, it brings victory to the child of God. As a matter of fact, lodged in the heart of the believer, in itself it becomes a power for holiness. Our Lord said to His disciples, "Already ye are clean because of the word which I have spoken unto you" (John 15:3). The apostle Paul, led of the Holy Spirit, spoke of the church as having been "cleansed . . . by the washing of water with the word" (Eph. 5:26).

Surely it must have been this conviction which

caused Moody to inscribe in the front of his Bible, "This Book will keep me from sin, or sin will keep me from this Book."

But perhaps you are saying, "It's very difficult for me to memorize the Word of God." Well, I would not say that memorization exhausts the meaning of the text of hiding God's Word in one's heart. On the other hand, I surely advocate the memorizing of Scripture. But suppose it is as you say, you learn it in the morning only to have forgotten it by evening. Nonetheless, it will be surprising how effective an instrument it is in the hands of God for your guidance and deliverance during the day. And furthermore, may I remind you of the purifying effect of that Word, which is good and wholesome and helpful.

A friend of mine has illustrated the effect of the Word of God by referring to the old splint baskets which some of us undoubtedly took on our picnics as well as to market. You will recall those baskets. They were made of strips of wood that were interwoven. My friend would speak of his memory as a sort of splint basket. He would imagine himself going down to the riverside to get a basketful of water, only to find as he raised the basket from the river that the water would pour out of the holes between the strips of wood.

"See," he would exclaim, "that's just exactly what I told you. I can't retain anything; I can't remember anything. It all just flows out."

Then, after those afflicted with faulty memory were somewhat encouraged to think that they had a compatriot, he would slyly add, "But wait a moment! At least the basket was cleaner after it had been put into the river and raised again."

So it is with our minds and hearts; the Scriptures do have a purifying effect. They can be most helpful, and they are most necessary if you and I are to live holy lives for God.

It may be helpful to some if we take the time at this point to look into the Word of God itself as an example of the use of Scripture in the matter of victory over the enemy. Surely there is no better illustration and no grander story to illustrate this truth than the narrative concerning our Lord's temptation. Without going into it fully, we can take one or two lessons from it which are of inestimable value.

The first lesson, which is very apparent, is that our blessed Lord repelled the tempter on each occasion by a quotation from the Holy Scriptures. You will notice that there was no attempt on the part of Satan to argue the issue involved in any specific quotation. True, there were other temptations; but, so far as those recorded for us are concerned, each seems to have been completely cared for by a single quotation.

I think most Christians would grant at once that the Lord Jesus Christ could well have uttered some word to Satan that would have repelled him, a statement which was not already in the Word of God. He was the Son of God, and surely it was not absolutely necessary that He turn to the pages of the Old Testament to find the answer to the tempter. Nevertheless He did, and the very fact that He placed such confidence in the sacred writings in the time of spiritual testing is evidence enough of the value that He placed upon the Word of God.

There is a second matter which we should in all honesty face, and that is the necessity of knowing the Word of God well enough to apply it to the specific instance involved. It is very true that the devil can quote Scripture for his purpose. As a matter of fact, in the record of the temptation we have an illustration of that very thing. A great deal could be said about the way Satan quoted Scripture. Undoubtedly it can be properly observed that he wrested the text from the context. Furthermore, he can be charged with stopping his quotation before it became very embarrassing to himself. For the very next verse declares, "Thou shalt tread upon the lion and adder, the young lion and the serpent shalt thou trample underfoot" (Ps. 91:13). However, our Lord made no response to this abuse of Scripture—this universal application to that which concerns only the one who abides under the shadow of the Almighty. Instead He simply quoted again from the Word of God, and it was sufficient.

Does not this reliance of our Lord upon the scriptures of the Old Testament in time of spiritual conflict set an example for us who claim to be His followers?

This provision for holy living is one which requires effort on our part to lay hold of. It is going to take the kind of consecration that will lead us to the reading and the study of the Word of God. It is my profound conviction that no Christian will know true holy living by indolence, by carelessness, by trying to find some shortcut to sanctification. Only a thorough giving of oneself to the revelation of God can lead to the kind of holiness that will be effective in the hands of the Lord in turning others to our blessed Saviour.

It is highly necessary, therefore, for the health of our own soul, that the Word of God occupy a large place in our life. The Word of God, deposited in our minds and hearts, can be used of the

Holy Spirit when a specific need arises. I am sure that on more than one occasion the Holy Spirit has brought to mind semi-forgotten scriptures, that we might be fortified and strengthened in the hour of need. I am equally sure that well-known and remembered Scripture passages have been brought to the minds of God's children in critical hours and have been used of God as their deliverance from depression, discouragement and disaster. It is highly important, therefore, that we regard the Word of God as tremendously significant.

True holiness of life will never result from a casual attitude toward the Holy Bible. While I would not want to say that God has not on occasion spoken definitely to an individual in a situation in which he finds himself when at random he has opened the pages of the Word of God and allowed his eyes to light upon a verse, yet it is my conviction that that is not the usual way of ascertaining God's will.

Perhaps the old story, apocryphal or otherwise, that has served to illustrate the dangers of this particular method, bears repetition. You will recall that a son of a godly mother went to another city. His good mother packed a Bible in his trunk. He noticed it upon unpacking in the strange city, but allowed it to remain in the

29

trunk. Only on an occasion of great struggle in his own life, in which he sensed his need for divine help, did he uncover the Bible and look at it. But, alas, he had not studied it—he did not know where to turn. Finally, in desperation, he allowed the Bible to fall open. Closing his eyes, he pointed out a verse with his finger. Alas and alack, the place where his finger rested said, "He went away and hanged himself" (Matt. 27:5). Even the unspiritual man realized that this was hardly an answer to his quandary, and he decided to try the expedient again. So, going through the same process, he put his hand upon the sacred page, opened his eyes expectantly and saw, "Go, and do thou likewise" (Luke 10:37). The young man was still fairly sure that this was not *the* answer, so he tried once more. This time to his consternation his hand rested upon the text, "What thou doest, do quickly" (John 13:27).

Of course, this story may be highly fictitious, but it does show the possibilities. It ought at least to serve as a warning that we should be acquainted with Holy Writ. We dare not take for granted our knowledge of the will of God apart from the study of God's Word.

I recall reading a sentence from George Henderson: "The Bible is unlike any other book, in that one must personally know its Author before one can really understand its contents; it resembles other books in that to be understood it must be read, to be known it must be studied."

If there is in our hearts any aspiration for holiness—if, implanted by the Holy Spirit, there is a deep desire for Christlikeness—then we can be absolutely sure that the Holy Spirit will lead us to make much of the Word of God. No one who has at his disposal the blessed Book of God and who neglects that Book can be a strong, holy Christian. What were those words D. L. Moody had in his Bible? "This Book will keep me from sin, or sin will keep me from this Book."

4

THE HEAVENLY FATHER'S
LOVING PROVISION:
CHASTISEMENT

MOST OF US probably do not like the word *chastisement*. The connotation it has for us is punishment for disobedience. While the word does have that meaning, and the Scripture so uses it, nevertheless I would remind you that the word *chastisement* in itself simply means child training.

I am quite sure that part of our heavenly Father's child training has nothing to do with willful disobedience on our part. More than one loving, obedient child of His has been allowed to go through the valley of the shadow or called to undergo testings of most serious kinds. Let us be sure of the fact that the presence of trial does not necessarily mean disobedience on the part of the one who is tried. Somehow in the alchemy of

God it is possible for trials to be transmuted into character.

However, when trials do come because of disobedience to our Lord, how thankful we should be. The Lord does discipline His children; He does not let us go off on any tangent we care to go. He is our heavenly Father; and just as we have had earthly fathers who cared for us—who sought to protect us from harm and to lead us in the paths of righteousness—even so, and to a greater extent, does our heavenly Father lead us and care for us and chastise us, when it is necessary.

To bring this subject before us in the language of Scripture, let us look at Hebrews 12: 5-11:

> My son, regard not lightly the chastening of the Lord, nor faint when thou art reproved of him; for whom the Lord loveth he chasteneth, and scourgeth every son whom he receiveth. It is for chastening that ye endure; God dealeth with you as with sons; for what son is there whom his father chasteneth not? But if ye are without chastening, whereof all have been made partakers, then are ye bastards, and not sons. Furthermore, we had the fathers of our flesh to chasten us, and we gave them reverence: shall we not much rather be in subjection unto the

33

Father of spirits, and live? For they indeed for a few days chastened us as seemed good to them; but he for our profit, that we may be partakers of his holiness. All chastening seemeth for the present to be not joyous but grievous; but afterward it yieldeth peaceable fruit unto them that have been exercised thereby, even the fruit of righteousness.

This passage of Scripture tells us many things about God's dealings with us, when in faithfulness He allows trials to come into our lives. So often when such circumstances arise we become hard, we complain, we grumble. This scripture is surely God's Word to us that we should not murmur, for God has a purpose in view when He allows chastisement to come.

There are at least three things here which I should like to emphasize in a particular way. Notice, first of all, this passage says that chastisement—allowing trial to come into our lives—is a sign of God's love, if we are truly His sons. Often our vision is so distorted, our reasoning so warped, that we think God hates us when He allows chastisement. But, no, this passage affirms very definitely that whom the Lord loves He chastens, and He scourges every son whom He receives.

In Revelation 3:19 we read: "As many as I

love, I reprove and chasten." Chastening then is an evidence of His love. That our Father wants us to be more like the Lord Jesus is certainly an evidence that He loves us; and furthermore, if chastening comes because of our disobedience, it surely is an evidence of His love. To let us go on in disobedience, to let us seek our own sinful and willful way and go farther and farther from the path of righteousness, would be tragic indeed; but God is a faithful Father and He is a loving Father.

I suppose all of us know something of what we are talking about because of our own experience. After all, we've all been children, and some of us have had the privilege of being parents. We know what it is to have our fathers after the flesh chasten us. I trust, in keeping with the Scripture, we learned to give them reverence. The question before us here is "Shall we not much rather be in subjection unto the Father of spirits?" Of course. For though we may not always be able to see clearly how His love is displayed in the providences of life, nevertheless we can be sure of His love; because, beyond any evidence that may come to us now, God has proved His love absolutely and clearly in that He gave His Son to be our Saviour.

But the passage in Hebrews tells us a second

thing: chastisement is a sign of our legitimacy. "What son is he whom his father chasteneth not? But if ye are without chastening, whereof all are partakers, then are ye bastards, and not sons." My friend, if you claim to be a Christian and there is no trial for you to face, no testings for you to go through, you may well look to it. This passage tells us that *all* of God's sons are partakers of chastening. As a matter of fact, chastening is the badge of our legitimacy.

There is a third matter brought to our attention in Hebrews 12. This matter has definitely to do with the subject we are considering. The question is posed, "Shall we not much rather be in subjection unto the Father of spirits, and live?" Chastisement is a sign of God's love, it is a sign of our legitimacy, but it is also permitted that we may truly know what it means to live. And what does it mean truly to live? It means our profit (v. 10). It means our being partakers of His holiness (v. 10). It means the fruit of righteousness (v. 11).

Life is not found in the countless round of pleasures that the worldling delights in, nor is life to be found in the possession of things. Life in essence is having a heart that is right with God. Life is characterized by righteousness, by holiness, by living for God. It is in these things that we find true satisfaction and do not have cause for regret. The Lord Jesus said, "I came that they may have life, and may have it abundantly" (John 10:10). The psalmist said, "Thou wilt show me the path of life: In thy presence is fullness of joy; in thy right hand there are pleasures for evermore" (Ps. 16:11).

Perhaps with me you will have to admit, and admit it sadly but nonetheless admit it, that it is often when suffering and trial come, when the hours are dark, that we turn most fully to God. So frequently the hour of prosperity finds us with a feeling of sufficiency. But, my friend, chastisement can change all that and make us sense our need of God. It is then that we truly live.

Let me remind you again that not all suffering is the result of a definite disobedience to God on the part of the sufferer. However, in some cases it is. Perhaps in your case there has been some open rebellion which you know about. Perhaps deliberately, willfully, you have walked the other way. Then thank God if His hand is heavy upon you. If, on the other hand, child of God, you may not know of any deliberate sin, of any rebellion against God in your heart, and yet you are suffering, then remember that God permits trials to come that we may live. It is always

God's purpose that we should be conformed more and more to the image of His Son.

I remember reading a story years ago, *The Sky Pilot,* written by Ralph Connor. Some of you may remember it. Mrs. Charles E. Cowman tells part of the story in her helpful *Streams in the Desert.* She tells about a lass by the name of Gwen. Wild and willful, Gwen had had her own way all her life. Then through a terrible accident she was crippled for life. She became very embittered and rebellious. On occasion the Sky Pilot (the minister) would visit her. On one of these occasions, seeing her in all her ill will and rebelliousness, he said that he wanted to tell her a story—a parable, he called it—the parable of the canyon. It went something like this:

Once there were no canyons on the face of the earth, only open, wild prairies, a great expanse. The Master of the prairie, the Lord, walking over His garden, looked on the great plains and said, "Where are your flowers?" The plains answered back, "Master, I have no seed." So the Lord spoke to the birds of the air, and they carried seeds of every kind and strewed them on the surface of the plains. Soon crocuses and roses and buffalo beans and yellow crowfoot and wild sunflowers and red lilies bloomed all the summer long.

One day, as the Master walked on His great prairie, He said, "Yes, I am well pleased, but where are the clematis and the columbine? Where are the violets and the windflowers and all the ferns and flowering shrubs?" So once again He spoke to the birds, and they carried the seeds and strewed them.

Then once more the Master had to ask, "Where are My loveliest flowers?" The prairie, so the storyteller related, cried sorrowfully, "O Master, I cannot keep the flowers. The wind sweeps so fiercely when the sun beats upon my breast that the seeds wither and fly away." So the Master spoke to the lightning, and with one swift blow the lightning cleft the prairie to the heart. The prairie rocked, groaned in agony, and for many a day moaned bitterly over the black, jagged, gaping wound in its breast.

But a river flowed and brought its waters and carried black mold. Once more the birds brought the seeds and dropped them in the canyon. After a long time the seeds grew, and vegetation decked out the rough walls with soft mosses and trailing vines, and covered the rocks with clematis and columbine. At the foot of the chasm grew trees, and at the foot of the trees grew violets, windflowers and maidenhair. It was the Master's favorite place.

The Sky Pilot told the story to Gwen. Then he said, "I'd like to read a verse of Scripture, and I'll change a word or two. 'The flowers of the Spirit are love, joy, peace, longsuffering, gentleness. . . .' Gwen, some of these flowers—these graces—grow only in the canyon."

Somehow the parable spoke to the heart of Gwen, and she asked, "Which are the canyon flowers, Sky Pilot?" He answered, "Gentleness, meekness, longsuffering." And Gwen sobbed, "There are no flowers in my canyon, only rough, rugged rocks." The Sky Pilot spoke assuringly, "Gwen, someday they'll grow."

You know, if we take as from the Lord the tragedy that comes, the sorrow that we know, the burden that we bear, God will cause these flowers to grow in us; because whom He loves He chastens, and scourges every son whom He receives, that we may become partakers of His holiness.

5

THE SON OF GOD'S GRACIOUS PROVISION: THE CROSS

A NUMBER OF YEARS AGO I shared a time of prayer with a number of brethren beloved in the Lord. In the company was my good friend, Dr. Addison C. Raws of Keswick, New Jersey. This brother led us in prayer and in the course of his address to God said something like this: "Lord, I thank Thee that Thou hast not made it easy to fail."

I must confess that I was immediately struck by the words, and I acknowledge that there was strong feeling that the statement was in error. After all, I saw a great deal of failure all about me. Beyond the failure that I saw about me was the fact that in my own life I certainly longed for far more of God than I had ever experienced. It seemed as though it was the easiest thing in the world to fail. But the more I thought about it, the more certain I was that I was wrong and that my brother was right. In spite of my failure and that of my fellow Christians to appropriate what God has for us, it is still true that He has made abundant provision for His children to live for Him. If no other impression is borne home upon your heart out of these chapters, I trust that the conviction that God has made lavish provision for you will abide with you.

May I remind you of the important statement made by the apostle Peter:

> Grace to you and peace be multiplied in the knowledge of God and of Jesus our Lord; seeing that his divine power hath granted unto us all things that pertain unto life and godliness, through the knowledge of him that called us by his own glory and virtue (II Peter 1:2-3).

Surely God has said exactly what He means, and this is what He said, namely, that He "hath granted unto us all things that pertain unto life and godliness." If there is anything I need for life, if there is anything I need for godly living, then God has already granted it to me. You will notice that this word of God is not a promise, it is not something that God says He will do in the future; it is something that is already done. He *hath* granted unto us all things that pertain unto life and godliness. I take it therefore that whatever our need is for holy living, God has already provided it.

The third of the provisions at which we are looking is the cross of our Lord and Saviour Jesus Christ. I would like to consider with you for awhile what may be called the fourfold meaning of the cross.

For a person to be a Christian at all, he certainly recognizes the first meaning of the cross, namely, that it is the place of atonement, the place of expiation for sin. What we are saying here is simply the old, old story of Jesus and His love. In short, it is the gospel message itself. God has pronounced sentence upon all men, in that all have sinned, and the wages of sin is death. The way of deliverance must be found somewhere beyond man. In the grace of God, He sent His Son into human history. The Lord Jesus Christ actually became man. He was born of the virgin Mary. He lived a life that completely honored God in every respect. His friends could say of Him, "who did no sin, neither was guile found in his mouth" (I Peter 2:22). Our Lord alone could face the multitude and issue the challenge, "Which of you convicteth me of sin?" (John 8:46). You know there was no response to that challenge, for no one could truly find any fault in Him.

Yet the fact of history is that Christ died. Such a death demands an explanation. If death is the

result of sin and the Lord Jesus Christ did not
sin, then the question must be What is the meaning of His death? The simple answer to that
question is the old gospel story—He took your
place, He took my place. This is no subtle theory of the atonement. It is the plain, clear statement of the Word of God. "Christ died for our
sins" (I Cor. 15:3) is the divine explanation.
Our blessed Saviour, who died on Calvary and
who the third day rose again from the dead, ever
liveth to save to the uttermost all who come unto
God by Him. I take it that we all know this
truth and that most of us received the blessed
Saviour some time ago. We know what it means
to be forgiven of our sins.

Thank God for the gospel of His grace which
brings forgiveness, eternal life, the blessing of
God to those who do not deserve it but who as
poor lost sinners plead only the precious blood
of Calvary. Here most certainly is the first meaning of Calvary. There is no use talking of any
other meaning unless we have embraced this
truth. There is nothing more for us here until
we have entered into this great salvation so lov-
ingly provided by our gracious God. It is a
simple matter that even now by faith you may
receive Him, if you have not already done so.
While all that is involved in the death of the

Lord Jesus Christ on Calvary is utter profundity, nonetheless God has ordained that the blessing may be received in the utmost simplicity. Says the apostle Paul, "By grace have ye been saved through faith; and that not of yourselves, it is the gift of God; not of works, that no man should glory" (Eph. 2:8-9).

Now, having established beyond any question of a doubt, I trust, the primary meaning of the cross in the redemption of men through the shed blood of the Lamb of God, we may go on in the Word of God to discover other truths connected with the cross of our Lord.

The second meaning of the cross has to do with the defeat of Satan, the great enemy of our souls. I trust that long ago you realized that the cross does not mark the defeat of the Son of God. Only stark unbelief would speak of Calvary as the untimely end of a good soul. Our blessed Lord did not die as a martyr; He did not even die merely to set before us the supreme example of devotion to principle. His death was not defeat. His death was glorious victory. To see how the Word of God itself views this cross of Christ as the place of triumph, it is necessary for us to look at several scriptures.

First of all, we turn to the prophecy in the Old Testament. As a matter of fact, it is the protevangelium, the first promise of the coming Redeemer. It was a word spoken by God to Satan, and yet within it is a great promise for men. Said our God, "I will put enmity between thee and the woman, and between thy seed and her seed: he shall bruise thy head, and thou shalt bruise his heel" (Gen. 3:15).

This very wonderful verse of Scripture, which has for centuries been regarded as Messianic, tells us an important fact concerning the cross. It is true that the Seed of the woman was bruised as to His heel; however, it should be noticed that He was to bruise the head of the serpent. The relative vulnerability of the head and the heel needs no word of explanation from me. The fact of the matter is from the very outset the Seed of the woman, the Son of God, born of the virgin Mary, was prophesied to be the victor. It is this fact that is behind the glorious assertion, "Calvary means victory."

Just before our Lord went to the cross He uttered a statement which definitely corroborates all that we have said concerning Genesis 3:15. The coming of the Greeks (John 12:20 ff.) seemed to be some kind of sign which our Lord understood as betokening the hour for which He had come into the world. He immediately spoke of His death. It is in that context that these words are to be found: "Now is the judgment of this world: now shall the prince of this world be cast out. And I, if I be lifted up from the earth, will draw all men unto myself" (John 12:31-32).

I would like to lay hold of just one of the three statements which our Lord made. He said, "Now shall the prince of this world be cast out." That the prince of this world is the antithesis of our Lord is made plain by our Lord's later statement, "I will no more speak much with you, for the prince of the world cometh: and he hath nothing in me" (John 14:30).

Our Lord did not look at the cross as the place of defeat; He regarded it as the place of triumph. The very basis of the eviction of Satan from his sphere of authority is the blood of the cross. It is true that Satan has asserted his supremacy. It is also true that the Bible speaks of him as the god of this age, as the prince of the powers of the air, as the prince of this world. The same blessed Book speaks of this world lying in the evil one (I John 5:19). However, let us make certain that the devil's dominion is not an everlasting one. Already he has been met in mortal combat and has been defeated. According to the Word of God, the happy day will come when he will be bruised under our feet (Rom. 16:20). According to the Word of God, the day will come when only one angel will be needed to execute the verdict that is already delivered, and Satan shall be bound in the abyss (Rev. 20:1-3).

But there is a third passage of Scripture which we should at least mention. It is the divine interpretation of the prophetic utterances at which we have already looked.

> And you, being dead through your trespasses and the uncircumcision of your flesh, you, I say, did he make alive together with him, having forgiven us all our trespasses; having blotted out the bond written in ordinances that was against us, which was contrary to us: and he hath taken it out of the way, nailing it to the cross; having despoiled the principalities and the powers, he made a shew of them openly, triumphing over them in it (Col. 2:13-15).

It is quite apparent that forgiveness (v. 13) has to do with Calvary. It is evident also that the cancellation of our indebtedness has to do with Calvary (v. 14). Equally true it is that the wonderful language of victory in verse 15 has to do with Calvary. At the cross there was the despoiling of the evil principalities and powers. At the cross there was the celebrating of the triumph of the Son of God over the evil forces of the devil. Many of you are aware that the last verb used in Colossians 2:15 has to do with the return of the victorious legions of an army, as in triumph they marched through the arch of triumph to the plaudits and acclaim of the multitude. You will recall, they dragged behind them the captives and spoils of the conquered people. It is that word which is used to describe the mighty triumph of the Son of God over Satan at Calvary.

It is apparent, therefore, that no child of God has to be beaten by the devil. The devil has great power, he has great authority which he has usurped for himself; but no child of God needs to be his victim. What does the Word of God say? "Be subject therefore unto God; but resist the devil, and he will flee from you" (James 4: 7). Will you notice that, before the devil is to be resisted, there is to be subjection unto God.

Again, "Be sober, be watchful: your adversary the devil, as a roaring lion, walketh about, seeking whom he may devour: whom withstand stedfast in your faith, knowing that the same sufferings are accomplished in your brethren who are in the world" (I Peter 5:8-9). But notice once again, there is an important injunction that precedes this matter of withstanding the evil one. You will find that command in verse 6: "Humble yourselves therefore under the mighty hand of God."

Again: "And they overcame him because of

the blood of the Lamb, and because of the word of their testimony; and they loved not their life even unto death" (Rev. 12:11). This one who is overcome by the children of God is none other than the devil and Satan, the deceiver of the whole world (v. 9). Notice here the stress upon the blood of the Lamb, which is the very foundation of the victory over Satan. The child of God is to take his stand in faith; he is to give his word of testimony. Furthermore, he is in utter consecration and dedication to God to put his devotion to the Lord even before life itself; namely, he is to love not his life even unto death.

It is apparent from these scriptures that victory over the evil one is based on the triumph of our Lord on the cross. His blood is the basis of victory. As God's children we may enter in on the basis of faith and surrender to the will of God.

The third meaning of the cross is perhaps best brought to our attention by asking the question Who died on the cross? Of course, our blessed Lord died on the cross; but who else died there?

Knowing this, that our old man was crucified with him, that the body of sin might be done away, that so we should no longer be in bondage to sin; for he that hath died is justified from sin. But if we died with Christ, we believe that we shall also live with him (Rom. 6:6-8).

The answer to our question is apparent from the quotation: "We died with Christ" (v. 8). Here we are led into a fact which we could not possibly know apart from divine revelation. It is the assertion of God that our old man was crucified with Christ, that we died with Christ.

In the Word of God a number of words are used to describe what man is by nature. The biblical expressions are *old man, body of sin, sin, flesh*. Three references will provide examples of these: Romans 6:6; 7:17; 8:3. The *old man* refers to what we were before the new birth. As Evan Hopkins reported Adolphe T. Monod's epigram, "The old man is the man of old." The *flesh* (when it has moral significance) has to do with the "self-life," the life—as suggested by Bishop Moule—which has self as its working center. The other expressions (*body of sin, sin*) emphasize the total depravity (extensively, not intensively) of the Adamic nature which each of us has.

Whatever the differences in meaning or emphasis of these words, it is our judgment that they all have one thing in common: they all refer to either the cause or the result of the operation of that principle of life (actually a principle of death) which is operative in man since the fall in Eden.

At this juncture we should look at a passage which incontrovertibly establishes the biblical fact that our nature is sinful. These verses place the Spirit and the flesh in contrast. The one is the antithesis of the other. God's Word says of believers: "who walk not after the flesh, but after the Spirit" (Rom. 8:4). There then follow these statements concerning the flesh: "the mind of the flesh is death . . . the mind of the flesh is enmity against God; for it is not subject to the law of God, neither indeed can it be: and they that are in the flesh cannot please God" (vv. 6-8).

It is clear from this passage of Scripture that man does not have divine life naturally; *death* is his natural state. It is therefore evident that such a man does not have the capacity to have fellowship with God, who is life. Moreover, this same scripture affirms that the mind of the flesh is not only hostile to God, but is hostility (enmity). It is utterly impossible for the flesh to be subject to the law of God.

The final, unequivocal statement of God is that "they that are in the flesh cannot please God." Our Lord Himself said, "That which is born of the flesh is flesh; and that which is born of the Spirit is spirit" (John 3:6). The only hope of man, therefore, is that he shall be "born of the Spirit." The new birth is the absolute essential.

Now, Romans 6 carries the divine assertion that the old man—which is energized by the Adamic principle of life, inimical toward God and not subject to God—was in God's sight crucified with the Lord Jesus Christ at the cross. At this juncture do not raise any question as to why this is so, how this is so, or what should be done about it. Let us simply face the fact and believe that what God says is true.

God's servant, the apostle Paul, entered into this truth and could say, "I have been crucified with Christ; and it is no longer I that live, but Christ liveth in me: and that life which I now live in the flesh I live in faith, the faith which is in the Son of God, who loved me, and gave himself up for me" (Gal. 2:20). Will you notice that in this verse of testimony the apostle Paul is definitely claiming exactly what he said God gave to him by revelation in Romans 6. Likewise you and I may definitely count upon God's Word as absolutely true, that in a judicial sense, in a positional sense, that which is antagonistic in me to God has been crucified with Christ.

The apostle Paul uses this truth in his presentation of the claims of God, for he wrote: "For the love of Christ constraineth us; because we thus judge, that if one died for all, therefore all died; and he died for all, that they that live should no longer live unto themselves, but unto him who for their sakes died and rose again" (II Cor. 5:14-15). Let us grant at once that there is something more than union with our Lord in death. Thank God there is also union with Him in resurrection. Of that we shall speak later. However, at this point we are speaking of the cross—what happened there—and it is the affirmation of God that our old man was crucified with Christ.

Having faced what God has actually said, we are now prepared to face what He says we should do in the light of the facts that He has revealed. Reduced to the very simplest of terms and the shortest of commands, there are two things which we are to do. First, we are exhorted to reckon ourselves to be dead indeed to sin but alive unto God (Rom. 6:11). Second, we are exhorted to present ourselves unto God as alive from the dead, and our members as instruments of righteousness unto God (Rom. 6:13).

You will notice that once again we have brought together two things which we have already seen, namely, faith and yieldedness. You and I are to reckon as true what God says is true. That involves faith. You and I are to present or yield our members unto God. That is surrender. An actual, absolute yielding of all that we are and have to God for His will, coupled with a living, wholehearted trust in Him to do what He promises to do—these are the keys which open the door to victory over self. That the child of God is to know such victory is indicated by Galatians 5:24, where that which is true characteristically is stated: "And they that are of Jesus Christ have crucified the flesh with the passions and the lusts thereof."

But there is a fourth meaning to Calvary, and one which completes the picture in giving us the full triumph of our Lord over all the enemies of the Christian. For many centuries the fathers of the church have taught that the world, the flesh, and the devil are the three foes which the Christian has to face. The cross deals with the devil and with self. Does it deal with the world? Indeed it does.

It is very interesting to look at Galatians 6:14 in the American Standard Version. "But far be it from me to glory, save in the cross of our Lord Jesus Christ, through which the world has been crucified unto me, and I unto the world." This passage clearly suggests that the cross of Christ becomes the place where the world is crucified to the believer and where the believer is crucified to the world.

The world of which we are talking is the world under the control of the evil one. It is of that world that God says, "Love not the world, neither the things that are in the world. If any man love the world, the love of the Father is not in him" (I John 2:15). The world has its appeal, its charm; and more than one Christian has, at least on occasion, succumbed to its temptations. The goddess of the world dangles before us all sorts of temptations. However, though they may be manifold in number, they are actually of only three kinds. These three kinds of temptations are clearly delineated for us in the Scripture itself.

The Word of God says, "For all that is in the world, the lust of the flesh and the lust of the eyes and the vain-glory of life, is not of the Father, but is of the world" (I John 2:16). There are only three things that this world, which is inimical to God, can offer us. They are pleasures, possessions, and position. The appeal to us is threefold: to our appetite, to our avarice, to our ambition.

The tragedy of our succumbing to these temptations is indicated in the classic utterance of Scripture, "And the world passeth away, and the lust thereof: but he that doeth the will of God abideth forever" (I John 2:17). All that is in the world that would seek to ensnare us, to take us out of the will of God to tread the forbidden paths which are proscribed by the Word of God, presents an overpowering temptation. How may we find deliverance? If the temptations should not be completely overcome by what is taught in I John 2, nonetheless there should be real hindrance set up. After all, the Scripture is plain that the world passeth away and the lust thereof.

In addition to the teaching of I John 2, let us return to Galatians 6:14. It is at the cross that all values take on their proper perspective. Looked at from Calvary, the solicitations to evil on the part of the world assume the hideous appearance which actually characterizes them. The world, which ridicules the cross of Christ, suddenly finds itself impaled on that very cross. The world becomes the repulsive thing it is to the spiritually sensitive soul who means business with God. That same Christian, though he may fear the allurements of the world and have no confidence in himself to face them, will, if he is utterly devoted to God and walking in faith, find that he need not fight the battle himself; he will find the world a crucified thing. He finds the ungodly world to be the thing it is actually—an object of scorn, a crucified thing. Similarly he finds that he is an object of scorn to the world; he becomes a crucified thing to it.

More than one of us, wondering how we would be received by those who have been our companions prior to our conversion, have had the answer without seeking very far. We have found that to live out-and-out for God, to take our stand in consecration and faith, means that the problem is solved of itself. It has not been a question of our giving up anybody; it has been a fact that we have already been given up.

Thus the cross in all its glory assumes transcendent importance in the victory of the child of God over the world, as well as over the flesh and over the devil. Isaac Watts has put it most beautifully in a stanza of his great hymn "When I Survey the Wondrous Cross."

> His dying crimson, like a robe,
> Flowed o'er His body on the tree;
> Then I am dead to all the globe,
> And all the globe is dead to me.

Is it any wonder that Augustus M. Toplady made his prayer:

> Rock of Ages, cleft for me,
> Let me hide myself in Thee;
> Let the water and the blood,

From Thy wounded side which flowed,
Be of sin the *double* cure,
Save from wrath and make me pure.

This blessed provision of God for triumphant living has been laid hold of by God's people. Thousands have been able to join Charles Wesley and sing:

He breaks *the power of canceled sin,*
   He sets the prisoner free;
His blood can make the foulest clean;
   His blood availed for me.

6

THE SON OF GOD'S GRACIOUS PROVISION: UNION WITH HIMSELF

THERE IS A GLORIOUS PARADOX in John 14:20. These two seemingly contradictory statements are given in the simplest of language. The words fell from the lips of our Lord Jesus Christ: "ye in me, and I in you."

Such a statement to one untaught by the Holy Spirit is a meaningless jumble of words. How is it possible for Christ to be in the believer and the believer to be in Christ? To one taught of the Holy Spirit, there is no inscrutable mystery in such a pronouncement. Acquainted as he is with the New Testament, and taught by the Spirit of God, he understands that he is in Christ (II Cor. 5:17; Eph. 1:1, 3; 2:10, 13; etc.). He also knows that Christ lives in him (Gal. 2:20; Col. 1:27; etc.).

The truth that the believer is in Christ is implicit in the prepositional phrase which is used in connection with the true exercise of faith toward the Saviour. The familiar John 3:16 says, "For God so loved the world, that he gave his only begotten Son, that whosoever believeth on him should not perish, but have eternal life." Those familiar with the language in which the New Testament was written know that the preposition quite literally is *into;* so that the clause reads, "whosoever believeth into him should not perish, but have eternal life."

We would not mislead the student of the Word of God in this regard, since it is true that there are other constructions used to indicate the exercise of faith. (Notice John 3:15; Acts 16:31; Rom. 9:33; and I John 3:23 as examples of different kinds of constructions used in the New Testament.) However, John's characteristic designation is as we have indicated (see John 3:16, 18, 36; 6:35, 40; 7:38, 39, 48; 8:30; 9:35, 36; 10:42; 11:25, 26, 45, 48; 12:11, 36, 37, 42, 44, 46; 14:12; 16:9; I John 5:10, 13). As a matter of fact, this same construction is used also in the book of Acts (see Acts 10:43; 14:23). The reason we take the time to point out this fact is that it seems to us highly suitable to indicate this meaning which is surely developed in the New Testament

61

—that believing is bringing us into Christ, so far as our position before God is concerned.

Furthermore, there is evidence to indicate that believing into Christ and believing Christ are not necessarily the same. "As he spake these things, many believed on him. Jesus therefore said to those Jews that had believed him, If ye abide in my word, then are ye truly my disciples" (John 8:30-31).

Since union with Christ not only means that we are in Him but also that He is in us, we should not be surprised to read of the two in one reference: "But as many as *received him,* to them gave he the right to become children of God, even to them that *believe on his name"* (John 1:12). This same truth is intimated in I John 5:11-12: "And the witness is this, that God gave unto us eternal life, and *this life is in his Son. He that hath the Son* hath the life; he that hath not the Son of God hath not the life."

Thus we have brought to our attention the blessed paradox of the Word of God. The believer is in Christ, and Christ is in the believer.

Let us first give attention to the teaching of the New Testament concerning our union with Christ. This union is applied to at least six different activities of our Lord.

In the first place, as we have already seen, the believer is united with Christ in His death.

Are ye ignorant that all we who were baptized into Christ Jesus were baptized into his death? (Rom. 6:3).

Our old man was crucified with him, that the body of sin might be done away, that so we should no longer be in bondage to sin (Rom. 6:6).

Because we thus judge that one died for all, therefore all died (II Cor. 5:14).

If ye died with Christ from the rudiments of the world, why, as though living in the world, do ye subject yourselves to ordinances (Col. 2:20).

For ye died, and your life is hid with Christ in God (Col. 3:3).

Who his own self bare our sins in his body upon the tree, that we, having died unto sins, might live unto righteousness (I Peter 2:24).

The second point of our union with Christ concerns His burial.

We were buried therefore with him through baptism into death (Rom. 6:4).

Having been buried with him in baptism (Col. 2:12).

In the third place, the believer is united with Christ in His resurrection.

63

For if we have become united with him in the likeness of his death, we shall be also in the likeness of his resurrection. . . . But if we died with Christ, we believe that we shall also live with him (Rom. 6:5, 8).

God . . . made us alive together with Christ . . . and raised us up with him (Eph. 2:4-6).

If then ye were raised together with Christ, seek the things that are above, where Christ is, seated on the right hand of God (Col. 3:1).

Faithful is the saying: For if we died with him, we shall also live with him (II Tim. 2: 11).

In the fourth place, we are united with Christ in His ascension.

[God] raised us up with him, and made us to sit with him in the heavenly places, in Christ Jesus (Eph. 2:6).

If then ye were raised together with Christ, seek the things that are above, where Christ is, seated on the right hand of God. Set your mind on the things that are above, not on the things that are upon the earth. For ye died, and your life is hid with Christ in God (Col. 3:1-3).

In the fifth place, we are definitely to be united with our Lord in His return.

When Christ, who is our life, shall be manifested, then shall ye also with him be manifested in glory (Col. 3:4).

In the sixth place, the Word of God indicates that we are united with our Lord in His coming reign.

If we endure, we shall also reign with him: if we shall deny him, he also will deny us: if we are faithless, he abideth faithful; for he cannot deny himself (II Tim. 2:12-13).

He that overcometh, I will give to him to sit down with me in my throne, as I also overcame, and sat down with my Father in his throne (Rev. 3:21).

Let us understand at once that this truth does not teach a confusion of the person of our Lord with the persons of those who are God's children. On the other hand, we can be certain that there is far more involved in this union than the relationship which exists between individuals in society. Probably the closest human relationship which could be used to illustrate the union of Christ and believers is the marital relationship. In this instance two individuals become one flesh. However, it should be observed that in our relationship to the Lord the union is even deeper and more wonderful. "The twain, saith he, shall become one flesh. But he that is joined unto the Lord is one spirit" (I Cor. 6:16-17).

This spiritual and vital union which connects us with our Lord guarantees our standing before God to be as perfect as His. Moreover, in this union is to be found a channel to His power for spiritual living.

This teaching of the Word of God should bring much assurance to our hearts and a sincere expectation that we can count not upon human energy, but upon supernatural power. The believer is in Christ.

Having made these observations, we have not exhausted the subject. The fact of the matter is, that Christ is also in the believer. Galatians 2: 20 is not meaningless jargon. Listen to the sacred words, "Christ liveth in me." It is in this very fact—that the living Christ lives in the child of God—that additional and wonderful hope is given to us for victory over sin. Let us remember that our blessed Lord is life, therefore the verses of the Word of God that present Him as our life are entirely correct.

This blessed truth is not merely unfolded in the New Testament, but actually is indicated in the Old Testament as well.

Jehovah thy God, . . . he is thy life (Deut. 30:20).

Jehovah is the strength of my life (Ps. 27: 1).

But what we see in the Old Testament is more clearly and explicitly set forth in the New Testament.

> For to me to live is Christ (Phil. 1:21).
> Christ, who is our life (Col. 3:4).
> It is no longer I that live, but Christ liveth in me: and that life which I now live in the flesh I live in faith, the faith which is in the Son of God, who loved me, and gave himself up for me (Gal. 2:20).
> I am . . . the life (John 14:6).
> Christ in you, the hope of glory (Col. 1:27).

Here is the great principle of life which sets forth the potential of all Christian living; namely, Christ lives in the believer. His resources are our resources. His power is most surely at our disposal. Whatever the circumstances of life— even if like Paul's they should involve a prison experience—we also can say, "To me to live is Christ." Christ is life to us.

Will you take notice of the fact that this presentation of Christian living is utterly above and beyond that which is the common conception. So often our kind of Christianity consists of externals, of rules and regulations contrary to our desires, of a standard of life that is so utterly difficult as to preclude the possibility of even approximating it.

Let us understand that Christianity does not only imply following the Lord Jesus, though following Him is involved in Christianity. Also, Christianity does not only imply trying to live like Christ, though every Christian should have the Lord Jesus Christ as his example. Furthermore, Christianity is not a series of doctrinal assertions to which we give assent, though every Christian does believe certain very definite things revealed in the Word of God.

A Christian is one who has received a Person. As a matter of fact, one of the distinguishing features of Christianity is that its Author is alive. But additionally, understand that the Author, the Lord Jesus Christ, actually lives in His followers. Here is something upon which we may count, of which we may be absolutely certain. Thank God for the encouragement that this truth brings. Praise God that the Son of God is ever present, not only with us, but in us. As in consecration and faith we look to Him, we shall find that He is the mighty Victor for us.

Let us remind you of two New Testament scriptures which, when believed, will help us to enter into the realization of Christ's presence in us, and of all that that truth should mean to us in holy living. The apostle Paul prayed "that Christ may dwell in your hearts through faith" (Eph.

3:17). Perhaps you wonder that the apostle Paul would pray that Christ would dwell in the hearts of those who were already believers. Does not the Word of God make plain that He has come to live in those who are truly His? Indeed so. Any question so raised will be settled if we understand the meaning of the word *dwell*. Perhaps it will be of help to us if we render the word "to be at home." The blessed Saviour, who lives in our hearts, wants to be at home in our hearts.

I need not tell you that it is possible to live in a place and not be at home. It does not take very much spiritual insight to understand that that which is contrary to the will of God, that which we know from the Word of God is opposed to God's will, will grieve our Lord. How could He be at home in a heart that grieves Him?

One of my beloved colleagues at Moody Bible Institute, the late Dr. Kenneth S. Wuest, teacher of New Testament Greek, has made this verse in his expanded translation to read, "That the Christ might finally settle down and feel completely at home in your hearts through faith."

The second passage of Scripture reads, "until Christ be formed in you" (Gal. 4:19). Here the great objective of Christ's indwelling is specifically stated that He shall be completely formed in us. Let us recall that we have been foreordained to be conformed to the image of God's Son (Rom. 8:29). To put it another way, the desire and the purpose of God involves for us "the stature of the fulness of Christ" (Eph. 4:13).

Now as we close our consideration of this important subject, let me draw to your attention two illustrations that set forth something of the wonder of these two marvelous truths that the believer is in Christ, and Christ is in the believer. The former of these truths is given grand and beautiful illustration in the teaching of our Lord concerning Himself as the vine. You will recall that He said, "I am the true vine. . . . I am the vine, ye are the branches" (John 15:1, 5). Without attempting any development of the wonderful truths given by our Lord in connection with this metaphor, let us simply stress here that He is teaching that the believer is in Him. Time was when I understood our Lord to mean, "I am the stem of the vine, ye are the branches." Long since I have discovered what He said was that He was *all*, He is the vine. You see, the branches are only part of the vine. The believer in Christ is truly in Christ.

J. Hudson Taylor has put the matter very beautifully.

As I thought of the vine and the branches, what light the blessed Spirit poured direct into my soul! How great seemed my mistake in having wished to get the sap, the fullness out of Him. The vine, now I see, is not the root merely, but all—root, stem, branches, twigs, leaves, flowers, fruit: and Jesus is not only that: He is soil and sunshine, air and showers, and ten thousand times more than we have ever dreamed, wished for, or needed.

The second illustration is taken from the Old Testament, and though it could be properly reserved for our dealing with the indwelling of the Holy Spirit, it nevertheless has application here. It is a word spoken of Gideon which says, "But the spirit of Jehovah came upon Gideon" (Judges 6:34). In the margin of the American Standard Version, a more literal translation of the Hebrew text is involved. It suggests, "The spirit of Jehovah clothed itself with Gideon." Permit me to change the neuter pronoun to the masculine, and capitalize two words: "The Spirit of Jehovah clothed Himself with Gideon." The believer is indwelt by Christ: I speak reverently —the believer is the clothing of the Lord Jesus Christ. He has clothed Himself with us.

O truth beyond description; O divine fact which utterly astonishes the human heart! God Himself is resident in the believer. What temptation is there that He cannot overcome? What circumstance is there in which He cannot be the victor? What need do I have that He cannot supply? Here is the source of true sanctification that, properly understood and earnestly believed, must result in growth in grace, in walking to please God more and more (cf. I Thess. 4:1) .

7

THE SON OF GOD'S GRACIOUS PROVISION: HIS PRESENT HEAVENLY MINISTRY

"For Christ entered not into a holy place made with hands, like in pattern to the true; but into heaven itself, now to appear before the face of God for us" (Heb. 9:24).

"It is finished" (John 19:30) may definitely be ascribed to the atoning work of our blessed Saviour. His sacrifice never needs to be repeated. His death upon the cross provided "a full, perfect, and sufficient sacrifice, oblation, and satisfaction for the sins of the whole world." However, let us remember that such an assertion does not mean that the Lord is not doing something for us now, nor is this present ministry to be limited to His living in the child of God. In corporeal form He is at the right hand of the Majesty on high. Hebrews 9:24 affirms that He is there "for us."

In His office as Mediator our blessed Lord ministers as Prophet, Priest and King. We understand that when our Lord teaches, He teaches as the royal and priestly Prophet; when He rules, He rules as the priestly and prophetic King; when He atones or intercedes, He is the prophetic and kingly Priest. Nevertheless, it is helpful for us to think of these three functions separately. Let us consider particularly His ministry as Priest.

As we have indicated, the propitiatory ministry of our Lord is complete.

> Now once at the end of the ages hath he been manifested to put away sin by the sacrifice of himself (Heb. 9:26).
>
> He, when he had offered one sacrifice for sins forever, sat down on the right hand of God (Heb. 10:12).
>
> By one offering he hath perfected forever them that are sanctified (Heb. 10:14).

But in addition, our Lord carries on a priestly ministry for His own now. This present ministry of our Lord in heaven is most intimately connected with our living for Him here. In this connection, there are two particular ministries which He carries on for us in His present priestly work. They have to do respectively with our need when we fail, and with divine provision for us even before we have to face temptation. These two ministries are those of advocacy and intercession.

More than one child of God has been greatly depressed in view of defection in his life. Perhaps he has succumbed to some temptation over which he thought he had the mastery. Suddenly, however, in the hour of testing, he finds that he has failed because he was not walking in fellowship with his Lord. What then? Listen to the Word of God: "My little children, these things write I unto you that ye may not sin. And if any man sin, we have an Advocate with the Father, Jesus Christ the righteous: and he is the propitiation for our sins; and not for ours only, but also for the whole world" (I John 2:1, 2).

It is well for us to remind ourselves that our blessed Saviour is faithful to us in the hour of our great need. Let us not add to Scripture, but let us rather believe exactly what it says; namely, that "if any man sin, we have an Advocate with the Father, Jesus Christ the righteous." Therefore, as soon as the child of God has failed, the Lord Jesus is ministering as his Advocate. Such loving ministry should melt our hardened hearts and cause us to want to live for Him completely. He is our Representative. He is the answer to

all the accusations of the devil. The pleading of
His blood is the full and final answer to any
question concerning the standing of the child of
God. With Charles Wesley we may say:

> Arise, my soul, arise!
>   Shake off thy guilty fears;
> The bleeding Sacrifice
>   In my behalf appears.
> Before the throne my Surety stands;
> My name is written on His hands.
>
> He ever lives above,
>   For me to intercede;
> His all-redeeming love,
>   His precious blood to plead.
> His blood atoned for all our race,
> And sprinkles now the throne of grace.
>
> Five bleeding wounds He bears,
>   Received on Calvary;
> They pour effectual prayers;
>   They strongly plead for me.
> "Forgive him, O forgive!" they cry,
> "Nor let that ransomed sinner die."
>
> The Father hears Him pray,
>   His dear anointed One;
> He cannot turn away
>   The presence of His Son.
> His Spirit answers to the blood
> And tells me I am born of God.

My God is reconciled,
   His pardoning voice I hear;
He owns me for His child,
   I can no longer fear.
With confidence I now draw nigh,
And "Father, Abba, Father!" cry.

God has provided that on the basis of what our blessed Saviour has done in the remission of our sins, we may find restoration and fellowship as we confess our sins. "If we confess our sins, he is faithful and righteous to forgive us our sins, and to cleanse us from all unrighteousness" (I John 1:9) .

When a child of God fails, he certainly does not need morbidly to dwell upon his defection. God grant that in true contrition and in deep repentance we may turn to the Saviour for restoration to fellowship. God help us to hate the sins that make Him mourn. But let us not stay in the place of a morbid introspection. Let us claim the merits of the blood of Christ. Let us believe God when He says that if we confess He will forgive. Let us believe the power of the blood of Christ to cleanse us from all sin.

Surely no child of God who has lived for even a brief while as a Christian needs to be reminded that our Lord's advocacy is a wonderful provision for us in this matter of holy living. Here is a provision that will give us courage so that, though we fall, we may rise again. But let us understand, and understand most definitely, that here is no excuse for sin. There is absolutely no antinomianism in this teaching of the Word of God. For a man to love his sin, to delight in hurting the One he calls his Saviour, is for him to disown the name of Christian, however vehement he may be in claiming the name for himself. The biblical Christian knows no other answer to the question, "Shall we continue in sin, that grace may abound?" than the vehement response of the apostle, "God forbid."

The second of our Lord's present heavenly ministries is that of intercession. "He ever liveth to make intercession for them" (Heb. 7:25). Perhaps this ministry of our Lord's is nowhere more graphically unfolded than in the blessedly wonderful words of Hebrews 4:14-16:

Having then a great high priest, who hath passed through the heavens, Jesus the Son of God, let us hold fast our confession. For we have not a high priest that cannot be touched with the feeling of our infirmities; but one that hath been in all points tempted like as we are, yet without sin. Let us therefore draw near with boldness unto the throne of grace,

78

that we may receive mercy, and may find grace to help us in time of need.

Our merciful and faithful High Priest knows our needs. As we go to Him, He can comfort our hearts and give us strength. Moreover, He intercedes on our behalf.

You will recall that on one occasion Peter was going to fail, and fail miserably; he was about to deny his Lord. However bold, however strong his assertions to the contrary, the word that the Lord said was going to be fulfilled. But our Lord was greatly concerned for Peter. Listen to the Scripture: "Simon, behold, Satan asked to have you, that he might sift you as wheat: but I made supplication for thee, that thy faith fail not; and do thou, when once thou hast turned again, establish thy brethren" (Luke 22:31-32).

How reassuring this word is. Our blessed Lord knows the end from the beginning. He knows, despite all the desires of our hearts, what is before us. To me it is of inestimable encouragement to know that He has already prayed for me. No circumstance of life catches Him unaware. He is able to anticipate, and He is our Intercessor who pleads for us.

One of the close associates of D. L. Moody was Major Daniel Webster Whittle. Major Whittle wrote the words to a number of gospel hymns.

Some of them carry his nom de plume, El Nathan. One which many of God's people have found most helpful was put to music by his daughter, May Whittle Moody, the wife of Will Moody. One of the stanzas with the refrain reads like this:

Never a heartache, and never a groan,
Never a teardrop and never a moan;
Never a danger, but there on the throne,
Moment by moment, He thinks of His own.

Moment by moment I'm kept in His love;
Moment by moment I've life from above;
Looking to Jesus till glory doth shine;
Moment by moment, O Lord, I am Thine.

So then we have strong encouragement from our Lord's present concern for us and His present ministry on our behalf. While there is some difference of interpretation, who is to question that involved in Romans 5:10 is the fact that our Lord's present ministry, His present life, is connected with our salvation from the power of sin. Says the text: "For if, while we were enemies, we were reconciled to God through the death of his Son, much more, being reconciled, shall we be saved by his life."

Many of us are familiar with the translation of Bishop Handley C. G. Moule: "For if, being enemies, we were reconciled by our God through the death of His Son, much more, being reconciled, we shall be kept safe in His life." The bishop went on to observe that the life of which he spoke was the life of the risen One who now lives for us and in us, and we are in Him. The bishop also emphasized the importance of the preposition "in" as over against "by." Our union with our blessed Lord is complete.

8

THE SON OF GOD'S GRACIOUS PROVISION: HIS RETURN

BIBLE-BELIEVING CHRISTIANS accept quite literally the predictions of the Word of God that our blessed Lord and Saviour Jesus Christ will come again. While such Christians frequently differ as to the time relation of that coming to certain other events predicted in the Word of God, they have been unanimous in their agreement that we are to expect a definite, personal, literal return of our Saviour.

It most certainly is not necessary for me to turn to a number of passages of Scripture in this connection. "This Jesus, who was received up from you into heaven, shall so come in like manner as you beheld him going into heaven" (Acts 1:11). "For the Lord himself shall descend from heaven, with a shout, with the voice of the archangel, and with the trump of God: and the dead in Christ shall rise first" (I Thess. 4:16).

Perhaps because of its very familiarity there should be added to these two quotations John 14:3: "And if I go and prepare a place for you, I come again, and will receive you unto myself; that where I am, there ye may be also." It may be observed concerning the last quotation, that whatever interpretation man may place on the present tense of the verb as indicated in the American Standard Version, the verse has been ordinarily associated with the coming of our Saviour. The list of teachers so instructing us is indeed imposing and includes such names as Origen, Calvin, Meyer, Hoffman, Luthardt, and Ewald. In any case, the great truth of the return of our Lord is part of the warp and woof of the fabric of the New Testament.

It is no wonder that the early church gave utterance to its earnest belief in the return of the Lord and Saviour. In the Apostles' Creed (while the creed does not date back to the time of the apostles themselves, no one would raise any question as to its real antiquity) the statement is "From thence He shall come to judge the quick and the dead." In the Nicene Creed (A.D. 325) the word is "And He shall come again with glory to judge both the quick and the dead." The symbol known as the Athanasian Creed (fifth or sixth century A.D.) contains this statement: "He ascended into heaven; He sitteth on the right hand of the Father God Almighty, from whence He shall come to judge the quick and the dead."

While there has not been uniform agreement among Evangelicals as to what men have been pleased to call the imminence of the return of the Lord Jesus Christ, nevertheless many believers of vastly different persuasions as to the details concerning the return of the Lord have agreed that the believer should expect the return of the Lord at any time—without setting any dates or insisting that it is mandatory for the Lord to come within his lifetime. While there are certain students of the Word of God who believe that certain known and observable events must occur before the Lord may come, even many of them hold in their hearts the hope of the possible return of the Lord in their own generation.

It is this expectation of the imminent coming of the Lord that caused Dr. A. A. Hodge to write:

> They [apostles] only taught (1) that it [the second advent] ought to be habitually desired, and (2) since it is uncertain as to time, that it should always be regarded as imminent.

It also led Dr. A. H. Strong to write:

The apostles . . . declared the knowledge of it [Christ's coming] to be reserved in the councils of God, that men might ever recognize it as possibly at hand, and so might live in the attitude of constant expectation.

These two quotations have been purposely chosen since they indicate the belief of those whose views were definitely conservative, and come to us from the past generation of American theologians. In addition, neither of these men was a premillenarian, with which school of interpretation the writer is very glad to identify himself. It is presumed that practically all premillenarians, however they may differ on the definition of the word *imminence,* would agree to the fact that the believer should be looking for the return of his Saviour.

I recall hearing a story about Robert Murray McCheyne when I was but a mere boy. The way in which the anecdote was told in America in those days was something as follows:

It was an evening. Gathered together at St. Peter's Presbyterian Church in Dundee was the session. Their spiritual young minister had evidently been reading deeply in the Gospel according to Matthew. There came a pause in the meeting and the young dominie looked full in the face of the man sitting next to him and inquired, "Do you believe that Christ may come tonight?" Rather taken by surprise, the man remained in silence for a few moments and then stuttered, "I—I don't think so." McCheyne spoke to the next man, posing the same question and receiving the same answer. One by one he asked each member of the session the same question and received the same reply. Then after a pause the young preacher opened his Bible and read: "Therefore be ye also ready: for in such an hour as ye think not the Son of man cometh" (Matt. 24:44).

It would seem as though McCheyne's word is entirely valid. Surely the Christian who is not looking for the return of his Lord is going to miss out in much of the blessing and of the provision that God has for those who wait for His Son.

With no thought as to a full development of the subject, may I simply remind you of certain facts concerning the coming of the Lord, particularly as His coming affects the believer in Christ. Beyond every other consideration for the believer, the coming of Christ ought to be an occasion of eager expectation, because it means that we shall be with the Lord.

In I Thessalonians 4, which deals with the fact of our Lord's return, there is this important word: "So shall we ever be with the Lord" (v. 17). Let me quote you two verses from Mr. Moody's favorite gospel hymn which express something of the glory which awaits us:

The King there in His beauty
    Without a veil is seen;
It were a well-spent journey,
    Though seven deaths lay between,
The Lamb with His fair army
    Doth on Mount Zion stand,
And glory, glory dwelleth
    In Immanuel's land.

The bride eyes not her garment,
    But her dear bridegroom's face;
I will not gaze at glory,
    But on my King of grace;
Not at the crown He giveth,
    But on His pierced hand;
The Lamb is all the glory
    Of Immanuel's land.

In the second place, the coming of our Lord reminds us that we shall be like Him. "We know that, if he shall be manifested, we shall be like him; for we shall see him even as he is" (I John 3:2). What mortal who loves the Lord does not long for the day of deliverance from infirmities? Says the Word of God, "Even we ourselves groan within ourselves, waiting for our adoption, to wit, the redemption of our body" (Rom. 8:23). "We wait for a Saviour, the Lord Jesus Christ: who shall fashion anew the body of our humiliation, that it may be conformed to the body of his glory, according to the working whereby he is able even to subject all things unto himself" (Phil. 3:20-21).

Furthermore, when our blessed Lord comes again, it means that we shall be gathered together with those we have loved long since and have lost a while. How infinitely precious are the words "together with them" (I Thess. 4:17).

Now, this subject of the coming of the Lord impinges on the matter of holiness. It seems to me that there are at least two definite applications. Let me suggest in the first place, that the whole teaching concerning the coming of our Lord gives meaning and honesty to the entire concept of the biblical idealism with which the Scriptures are filled. If we are forever to attain the experience of godly living only very imperfectly, then it seems to me we fall far short of the hope which has been placed in our hearts by the Word of God. The doctrine of the second coming of our Lord is essential to the perfection of Christianity itself. It is at the return of our Lord, according to the Scriptures, that we shall lay hold of that for which we have been laid hold on by Christ Jesus. There is perfect realization ahead.

The pragmatist, who frowns upon the idealist because the latter is living with his head in the clouds, and the idealist, who frowns upon the pragmatist for being so earth-bound, do not have the final answer in either case. The biblical eschatology gives reason to the biblical idealism; for while the child of God can know something of the life that wins now, the full realization, the full attainment of that ideal, awaits the time when we shall see our blessed Saviour. Meanwhile, we can say with a friend of ours, "I am not all that I ought to be; I am not all that I'm going to be; but, thank God, I am not what I used to be."

There is a second relationship between the doctrine of the return of Christ and the subject of holiness, and that concerns our living for God now. You see, this matter of expecting the Lord to come should make a difference in the way we live. Let us allow the Scriptures to speak deeply to our hearts.

We know that, if he shall be manifested, we shall be like him; for we shall see him even as he is. And everyone that hath this hope set on him purifieth himself even as he is pure" (I John 3:2-3).

Denying ungodliness and worldly lusts, we should live soberly and righteously and godly in this present world; looking for the blessed hope and appearing of the glory of the great God and our Saviour Jesus Christ (Titus 2: 12-13).

The heavens shall pass away with a great noise, and the elements shall be dissolved with fervent heat, and the earth and the works that are therein shall be burned up. Seeing that these things are thus all to be dissolved, what manner of persons ought ye to be in all holy living and godliness, looking for and earnestly desiring the coming of the day of God. . . . Wherefore, beloved, seeing that ye look for these things, give diligence that ye may be found in peace, without spot and blameless in his sight (II Peter 3:10-12, 14).

If any man would come after me, let him deny himself, and take up his cross, and follow me . . . for the Son of man shall come in the glory of his Father with his angels; and then shall he render unto every man according to his deeds (Matt. 16:24, 27).

In each of these quotations the idea of the coming of the Lord or some associated eschatological event is connected with the theme of holi-

ness. The apostle John **speaks** of the coming of
the Lord as an event which should involve the
believer's setting his hope on the Lord. Part of
that hope is that the believer shall be like the
Lord when he sees Him.

The "if" of the American Standard Version
(I John 3:2) should not mislead us. It is an ac-
curate translation of the original. It should be
understood that the "if" does not raise any question as to the fact of the Lord's coming; it only
suggests that we do not know when He will
come. We should so live that if He should be
manifested now, not only should we know that
we shall be like Him in His coming, but we
should be so living as to meet His approval. Ear-
lier in the epistle the apostle spoke of the possibility of being ashamed before the Lord at His
coming (I John 2:28). Consequently in this passage in chapter 3, he reminds us that if our hope
is truly on the coming Lord, then without question "everyone that hath this hope set on him
purifieth himself, even as he is pure."

The proper attitude toward the return of the
Lord, therefore, results in purity of life. If we
properly understand what our Lord desires of
us and all the provision He has made for us to
realize His purpose, then we shall want to give
ourselves in utter surrender and walk in faith

each day of our lives. He is coming again and we shall give answer to Him. Both because of our love for Him and our sense of accountability to Him, we shall certainly want to live as He wants us to live.

The apostle Peter not only stresses the fact that the heavenly and earthly things which we see are temporal—and therefore should not be the supreme object, the final goal of our living upon earth—but he also suggests that we look for new heavens and a new earth. Now both these matters, the dissolution of the present world system and the creation of the new heavens and the new earth, argue for holiness of life. Says the apostle Peter, "Seeing that these things are thus all to be dissolved, what manner of persons ought ye to be in all holy living and godliness?" (II Peter 3:11). Concerning both the dissolution of the present heavens and the creation of the new heavens and the new earth he says, "Seeing that ye look for these things, give diligence that ye may be found in peace, without spot and blameless in his sight" (II Peter 3:14).

The apostle Paul tells us that the same grace of God, which has instructed us to deny ungodliness and worldly lusts and to live soberly and righteously and godly in this present world, also teaches us to look for the blessed hope and appearing of the glory of the great God and our Saviour Jesus Christ. It is apparent that looking for the blessed hope is a contributing force and factor in the realization of practical holiness, which involves denying ungodliness and worldliness, and living soberly and righteously and godly.

Our blessed Lord, in the quotation from Matthew 16, makes very plain the connection between denying oneself, taking up one's cross and following Him, on the one side, and the coming of the Lord, on the other side. Why should a man be willing to deny himself, to take up his cross and to follow the Lord? The Lord gives three reasons, each introduced by the little word *for*. The last of these three reasons is that the Lord Jesus Christ is coming again and God's children are responsible to give an account to Him, for, says the Scripture, "then shall he render unto every man according to his deeds" (Matt. 16: 27).

My friend, what about the coming of the Lord? Is it simply a theoretical matter upon which to speculate, so far as you are concerned? Perhaps impertinently may I ask the question, Are you more concerned about the details of prophecy and proving the validity of the intricacies of your own position than you are about considering the fact that you are actually going to meet the Lord and give an account to Him? I would be the last one to minimize the importance of a very thorough and careful study of the Word of God and of the relating of one passage of Scripture to another; nevertheless, I make bold to suggest that first of all the coming of the Lord must mean to us that we are going to see Him and that we are going to give an account to Him. If this particular fact concerning the return of the Lord assumes a large place in our lives, it is going to make a difference in the way we live. The hope itself will become what God means it to become, namely, a purifying hope. Here is one of God's provisions for holy living.

The coming of the Lord can become a great shield to us—a guard to our lips and to our feet and hands. Moreover, I believe that, when this truth is lodged in our hearts, there is a liberating power from God Himself that truly makes it the purifying hope that the apostle John speaks about.

Those of us who had the privilege of knowing Dr. W. H. Griffith Thomas will not soon forget his constant reminder, as he spoke on the theme of the return of our Lord, as to what our attitude should be toward that coming. He used to say there are four words which should characterize our attitude toward the coming of our Lord and Saviour. The first word is *wait*—"to wait for his Son from heaven" (I Thess. 1:10); the second word is *watch*—"let us watch and be sober" (I Thess. 5:6); the third word is *expect*—"the earnest expectation . . . waiteth"; "ourselves also . . . waiting for our adoption" (Rom. 8:19, 23); the fourth word is *love*—"all them that have loved his appearing" (II Tim. 4:8).

When He shall come resplendent in His glory,
　　To take His own from out this vale of night,
O may I know the joy of His appearing,
　　Only at morn to walk with Him in white.

When I shall stand within the court of heaven,
　　Where white-robed pilgrims pass before my sight;
Earth's martyred saints and blood-washed overcomers,
　　These then are they who walk with Him in white.

When He shall call from earth's remotest corners
　　All who have stood triumphant in His might;
O to be worthy then to stand beside them,
　　And in that morn to walk with Him in white.*

ALMEDA J. PEARCE

*Used by permission of the author, Mrs. Pearce.

9

THE HOLY SPIRIT'S BENEFICENT PROVISION: THE CREATION OF THE NEW MAN

THE BIBLE makes it clear that God operates in that spiritual experience which the theologians call regeneration. "Of his own will *he brought us forth* by the word of truth" (James 1:18). "According to his mercy *he saved us,* through the washing of regeneration" (Titus 3:5). That it is God the Holy Spirit who is operative in the new birth is made plain by the teaching of our Lord. He said, "Except one be born of water and the Spirit, he cannot enter into the kingdom of God. That which is born of flesh is flesh; and that which is born of the Spirit is spirit" (John 3:5-6).

This regenerating work of God the Holy Spirit is a work of creation: "Wherefore if any man is in Christ, there is a new creation" (II

Cor. 5:17 marg.). Elsewhere the Bible speaks of this creation as a new man: "That ye be renewed in the spirit of your mind, and put on the new man, that after God hath been created in righteousness and holiness of truth" (Eph. 4:23-24). "[Ye] have put on the new man, that is being renewed unto knowledge after the image of him that created him" (Col. 3:10). We therefore in this study would like to look at the biblical teaching which concerns the creation of this new man, and some of its implications.

At the outset it is necessary to make crystal-clear that the creation of the new man is no guarantee that the Christian will live a life of victory, or else every truly regenerated person would do so automatically. Thus this provision is not to be thought of in precisely the same manner as we think of the other provisions. But having said that, let us not mistake the importance of this provision of God, nor think of it as an unnecessary appendage. It is true, as Evan Hopkins has said, "The power of the 'new man' is not sufficient to overcome the power of the evil nature." Nevertheless there is most certainly some connection between the creation of this new man and the possibility of living for the Lord. If that relationship is doubted, we may simply ask the question Why did God create the new man? In

97

this study we are concerned about two matters: (1) What is this new man? (2) What is his relationship to the victory of the child of God?

Let me confess at once that this subject is large and profound. I do not have all the answers. However, I believe there are some very definite statements in the Word of God. Further, I believe certain conclusions may be reached from these statements in the Holy Bible. So, however many problems may remain in the realm of metaphysics, let us address ourselves to the Word of God.

As we approach such a consideration, it should be kept in mind that the antithesis of the new man is that which the Bible calls the old man. We have already looked at a passage of Scripture in which this expression occurs. You will recall that the old man stands for all that we were before the new birth. The term brings before us as its activating principle, its life, the Adamic nature. We understand that that which is antagonistic to God, that which is not subject to God in us, has, in the estimation of God, been crucified with Christ. God in His Word asks us to reckon on that fact.

Concerning this old man, the Word of God says that it "waxeth corrupt after the lusts of deceit" (Eph. 4:22). In contradistinction to the old man, the new man is definitely described as the creation of God, "that after God hath been created" (Eph. 4:24); "the new man, that is being renewed unto knowledge after the image of him that created him" (Col. 3:10). Furthermore, this new man is said to have been created "in righteousness and holiness of truth" (Eph. 4:24). Another matter of more than passing significance is the reference to renewing: "that ye be renewed in the spirit of your mind" (Eph. 4:23); "that is being renewed unto knowledge" (Col. 3:10).

According to our understanding of the teaching of the Word of God, regeneration does not substitute another creation for the substance or the essence of a soul. However, regeneration or the new birth does produce a moral change, in disposition, in character, in the direction of the soul's activities; a new principle of life is infused; spiritual life is imparted. The believer, in short, has new life; he has put on the new man (Col. 3:10).

While it is hardly necessary at this point to enter deeply into the subject, it may be observed in passing that it is surely incorrect to come to the conclusion that in the believer there are two different individuals, two persons. We recognize then that if the word *nature* is used, it is not synonymous with the word *person*. We would particularly caution against the believer's regarding the old man as an *alter ego* that he can blame for his sin as though that nature were distinct from himself. If not in so many words, it would seem that some in their attitude say, "I am not responsible for my sin. The new man did not sin, the old man did it all—what else could be expected?" Let us beware of even the semblance of antinomianism. We dare not sit back and say that sin cannot be helped because we have this old nature—as though that excused us.

It would seem best to me to think of the old man and the new man as activated by two principles, two dispositions, two elements—the one of death, the other of life. Both of these principles are present in the believer.

A further word of warning may be wise. The common idea of the supremacy of the good over the bad, the triumph of the upper nature over the lower nature, is not biblical teaching. Let us understand that nothing less than the indwelling Christ can deliver us from the bondage of sin. We must come to the place where it is no longer I, but Christ, if we are to enter into the fullness of Christian living.

However, though victory is not to be found in the battling for dominance by the new man over the old, there are certain guarantees to us on the basis of this new life which we have from God. First of all, may I suggest that the very possibility of progressive sanctification is involved in the believer's having this new man. True, the work of progressive sanctification is wrought by God, the Holy Ghost. True, He uses the means of grace to enable us to grow. But there must be in us that which can respond to God.

The old man is deserving only of crucifixion. Moreover, of the man who is unregenerate, who is in the flesh, the Word of God says:

> For the mind of the flesh is death; but the mind of the Spirit is life and peace: because the mind of the flesh is enmity against God; for it is not subject to the law of God, neither indeed can it be: and they that are in the flesh cannot please God (Rom. 8:6-8).

> Now the natural man receiveth not the things of the Spirit of God: for they are foolishness unto him; and he cannot know them, because they are spiritually judged (I Cor. 2:14).

Consequently, unless we have been quickened of the Holy Spirit, unless there has been the principle of a new life implanted in us, there is no possibility for growth in grace.

In the second place, may I suggest that the

very possibility of understanding the Word of God at all rests in the creation of this new man. True, we must have the teaching of the Holy Spirit of the divine revelation. But since spiritual things are spiritually understood, and since the natural man cannot understand spiritual things, the believer must have a capacity for spiritual knowledge. It seems to me that this fact is involved in the stress of the texts at which we have already looked, in such assertions as "the new man, that is being renewed unto knowledge after the image of him that created him" (Col. 3:10); "that ye be renewed in the spirit of your mind, and put on the new man" (Eph. 4:23-24). And in this connection we should remember the very familiar words of Romans 12:2: "Be ye transformed by the renewing of your mind."

In the third place, let us thank God that we do have a new man which loves the things which God loves and hates the things which God hates. For, mark it well, this new man has been created "in righteousness and holiness of truth" (Eph. 4:24). Moreover, this new man "is being renewed unto knowledge *after the image of him that created him*" (Col. 3:10). Thus we have had created in us divine life, God's own kind of life, and though victory is not thereby ensured, we do have the capacity for relationship to the

Lord and for receiving the teaching of His Holy Spirit.

However, there is no teaching of the Word of God concerning the fruit of the new man. There is no word about the new man being life to us. It is the fruit of the Spirit (Gal. 5:22-23). It is the life of Christ (Rom. 8:11; Gal. 2:20; Phil. 1:21).

10

THE HOLY SPIRIT'S BENEFICENT PROVISION: HIS INDWELLING AND HIS FULLNESS

ONE OF THE MOST amazing facts concerning Christianity is the clear teaching of the Bible that God Himself comes to dwell in the one who trusts in the Lord Jesus Christ. Said the Lord Jesus, "If a man love me, he will keep my word: and my Father will love him, and we will come unto him, and make our abode with him" (John 14:23).

We already have looked at several passages of Scripture. Remember, "Christ in you, the hope of glory" (Col. 1:27), and "Christ liveth in me" (Gal. 2:20). Recall as well the words of our Lord in His high-priestly prayer, "I in them" (John 17:23).

That the God of high heaven should condescend to dwell in the human heart is indeed a wonder of amazing proportions. Yet is not this His promise even from olden time? "For thus saith the high and lofty One that inhabiteth eternity, whose name is Holy: I dwell in the high and holy place, with him also that is of a contrite and humble spirit, to revive the spirit of the humble, and to revive the heart of the contrite" (Isa. 57:15).

Great indeed were the edifices erected of old to various gods, yet of some of the most remarkable ever built by man the apostle Paul affirmed, "The God that made the world and all things therein, he, being Lord of heaven and earth, dwelleth not in temples made with hands" (Acts 17:24). Though we may be greatly impressed by the temples erected by man, some of which were colossal and remain as impressive reminders of the devotion of men to their gods, God chooses to dwell in the temple of the human heart.

We are all quite conscious that it is the third Person of the blessed and adorable Holy Trinity who is most frequently spoken of as coming to dwell in the heart of the one who believes in the Lord Jesus Christ. Our blessed Lord Himself promised that the Holy Spirit would so come:

> And I will pray the Father, and he shall give
> you another Comforter, that he may be with
> you forever, even the Spirit of truth: whom the
> world cannot receive; for it beholdeth him not,
> neither knoweth him: ye know him; for he
> abideth with you, and shall be in you (John
> 14:16-17).

Mighty indeed were the evidences of the presence of the Spirit of God coming upon the worthies of the Old Testament. It could be literally said of them that the Holy Spirit was with them. But here in John 14 our Lord announces a more profound truth, a more amazing fact. He says, "He abideth with you, and shall be in you."

But perhaps you think this blessing is something reserved for apostles or for those whom you consider the élite of the church. May I remind you that of a group of Christians who could not be said to be stalwart, spiritual believers in Christ there is a statement made which leaves us in no doubt. Granted that the Corinthian Christians had many gifts, nevertheless, you will recall that the apostle Paul had to speak to them as unto carnal (I Cor. 3:1-3). It was to these carnal believers that Paul directed this question, "Know ye not that your body is a temple of the Holy Spirit which is in you, which ye have from God? and ye are not your own; for ye were bought with a price: glorify God therefore in your body" (I Cor. 6:19-20).

There are other passages which appear to be parallel to I Corinthians 6:19-20. However, there are those who believe that the other verses have particularly to do with the body of Christ, namely, the church. I have in mind these verses:

> Know ye not that ye are a temple of God, and that the Spirit of God dwelleth in you (I Cor. 3:16). For we are a temple of the living God; even as God said, I will dwell in them, and walk in them; and I will be their God, and they shall be my people (II Cor. 6:16).

Whatever may be your interpretation of these passages, there surely can be no doubt as to the meaning of I Corinthians 6:19-20. The very use of the personal pronoun "your" seems to establish the fact that the church is not the subject of this passage. It is the believer's body that is a temple of the Holy Spirit, and the Holy Spirit is in the believer. Granted that the pronouns are plural, nevertheless, it seems evident that the apostle is speaking of the profound truth of the Holy Spirit's indwelling of each child of God. The context with its emphasis upon personal purity (vv. 15-18) would seem to establish the point.

Do you need more evidence? Then listen to this amazing and wonderful declaration. I confess that this particular passage of Scripture has meant a great deal to me and God has used it to speak deeply to my own heart. "And because ye are sons, God sent forth the Spirit of his Son *into our hearts,* crying Abba, Father" (Gal. 4: 6). May I remind you of another occurrence of the words "in our hearts." I refer to II Corinthians 1:22: "[God] sealed us and gave us the earnest of the Spirit in our hearts." Surely there can be no question raised, for the Word of God clearly teaches that the Holy Spirit has come to take up His residence in the heart of the child of God. Says the apostle Paul, "Ye are not in the flesh, but in the Spirit, if so be that the Spirit of God dwelleth in you. But if any man hath not the Spirit of Christ, he is none of his" (Rom. 8: 9).

Perhaps we should not leave this subject without at least rehearsing one glorious passage from the Gospel according to St. John.

Now on the last day, the great day of the feast, Jesus stood and cried, saying, If any man thirst, let him come unto me and drink. He that believeth on me, as the scripture hath said, from within him shall flow rivers of living water. But this spake he of the Spirit, which they that believed on him were to receive: for the Spirit was not yet given; because Jesus was not yet glorified (John 7:37-39).

Here is a tremendous spiritual truth which, when laid hold upon and believed, will make all the difference in the world in our Christian living. May I remind you that in this truth itself there is a great expulsive power. The very fact that the Holy Spirit is living in me will make a difference in the way I live. You see, there are some things that I cannot do with propriety. There are some places where I just will not go when I realize that this body of mine is truly the temple of the Holy Spirit. As a matter of fact, the passage I Corinthians 6:19-20 joins hard upon the fact that the Christian is to live a life of purity. There is something incongruous, there is something utterly improper, in prostituting that which is the temple of God for base and sordid purposes.

I recall a good many years ago talking to a very good friend and teacher of mine, a man whom God used in a remarkable way to bring to my heart both the truth of the victorious life and the responsibility for worldwide missions. That man's name was L. L. Legters. I recall that he spoke to me out of his heart one day and said something like this: "I have tried to make it a practice in my life, upon awaking each morning, even before I get out of bed, to raise my heart in prayer to God and to thank Him that my body is the temple of the Holy Spirit."

Now, what my friend was doing was to appropriate with God's help this great truth which in itself has a great expulsive power. I remember, therefore, that God is living in me. Oh, that we would dare to believe Him. Oh, that we would dare to take this truth not as something theoretical, but as presenting an absolute, actual fact. My friend, this is not imagination. This is not daydreaming. This is the truth of the Word of God. My body, your body—if we are Christians— is indwelt by none other than the Holy Ghost.

Now, having looked at the fact of the Holy Spirit's indwelling and the elementary and most apparent application of the truth to holy living, let us look a bit more deeply into the subject. Let me put it this way. It seems to me that we can say the work of the Holy Spirit's indwelling the child of God is to live the life of Christ in the believer. Yes, I am quite sure that He directs our minds and hearts in reading, in meditating, in studying the Word of God. Moreover, I am sure that He brings to our remembrance that which we have read, and will empower us in our service for God. As a matter of fact, all true Christian service is not only Holy Spirit-inspired, it is also Holy Spirit-energized. It is not what I do for God that counts, it is what God does in and through me (Phil. 2:13). But I wonder if we have not said the whole thing, at least in embryo, when we have affirmed that it is the purpose of the Holy Spirit to live the life of Christ in the believer.

When the apostle Paul, led of the Spirit, wrote about the work of the Holy Spirit in the child of God, he spoke of that work as "the fruit of the Spirit" (Gal. 5:22). You will recall what this fruit is. In contradistinction to the works of the flesh, there is the fruit of the Spirit. One cannot help but notice the difference between the plural and the singular number of the words.

The fruit of the Spirit is love, joy, peace, long-suffering, kindness, goodness, faithfulness, meekness, self-control. Now what about these nine virtues which constitute the fruit of the Spirit? Are they not, in short, simply the life of Christ? Can you imagine a more able or a fuller presentation of the character of our blessed Lord than these wonderful virtues which are the fruit of the Holy Spirit?

But wait, my friend, it seems to me the very wording here is a suggestion of deep significance. Take that word *fruit*. What does it mean? What does it connote? Every one of us knows that fruit can never be borne until there is death. Said the Lord Jesus, "Verily, verily, I say unto you, Except a grain of wheat fall into the earth and die, it abideth by itself alone; but if it die, it beareth much fruit" (John 12:24). It becomes apparent at once, therefore, that what we are talking about is not a human struggle of self-effort for holiness. It is not Christian character manufactured by dint of human prowess. Here is a work of the Holy Ghost that comes to pass when first of all there is death.

The work of the Holy Spirit in His indwelling is possible only as He fills our hearts and our lives. The apostle Paul was not speaking meaningless jargon when he said, "Be not drunken with wine, wherein is riot, but be filled with the Spirit" (Eph. 5:18). Though we may be theologically correct, what value has that if we do not know the presence of the Holy Spirit in power. It seems to me that the most needful message for the church today concerns this very matter of the fullness of the Holy Spirit. We have a great deal of activity. We even have some moving of the blessed Holy Spirit. But who would dare say that we know anything of what it would mean to have even a few who knew the fullness of the Holy Ghost.

In the days when it was my privilege to be a pastor, I affirmed on more than one occasion to my people that if God would give us even a handful of people who really mean business with Him, who would go all out for the Lord, who would in utter surrender and absolute faith walk with the Lord, the ends of the earth would feel the impact of that kind of living. We need Christians full of the Holy Ghost.

But before we shall know His presence in fullness and in power, there will have to be confession of sin, and such a confession of sin that includes contrition and restitution. Let me read to you from the Word of God: "Having therefore these promises, beloved, let us cleanse ourselves from all defilement of flesh and spirit, perfecting holiness in the fear of God" (II Cor. 7: 1).

"Let us cleanse ourselves." You and I are not able to provide the ground of that cleansing; we do not have to. The Lord Jesus shed His precious blood on Calvary for that cleansing. But you and I do have to provide the instrument by which this daily cleansing will be ours, and that instrument is confession. "If we confess our sins, he is faithful and righteous to forgive us our sins, and to cleanse us from all unrighteousness" (I John 1:9).

I believe that if we are to know fellowship with God—that fellowship with God that will make us live as we ought to live, that will give us the character we should have, and that will make us the servants of God we should be—we must confess our sin, any sin that comes between us and God. We cannot put a lid on it, we cannot extenuate it, we cannot in any way go on with God while sin remains unconfessed and harbored in our hearts. "Let us cleanse ourselves."

Do you remember how this matter is put in the book of Acts? "He made no distinction between us [the Jews] and them [the Gentiles], cleansing their hearts by faith" (Acts 15:9). When by an act of faith in the Lord Jesus I claim that forgiveness of God for sin, there is fellowship, unbroken and complete, between me and the holy God.

To prove the validity of that confession, I think there ought to be contrition. As I look into this cold heart of mine, I realize that if there is any sin above another sin it is the sin of hardness of heart—a heart that is unwilling to melt and eyes that are unwilling to cry. I know that we live in the Occident. I understand that the Western world prides itself on its ability to restrain its feelings, to be undemonstrative; but oh, that we might cry for our sins and for the

114

sins of the world! Somehow or other, I think we would get farther. I think these hearts of ours would not be so hard, so complacent.

But beyond that—to me this is absolutely necessary, and I do not think the reality of confession can be demonstrated to man apart from this—there is restitution. That is the proof that, when I say I am sorry, I really am. When it is within our power to make right the thing we have done wrong, God help us to make it right! If we want the fullness of the Spirit of God, it begins right here—but it does not end here.

There is a second thing that is absolutely necessary—consecration, yieldedness to God, surrender to the Lord. I wonder, Christians, as we face the issue right now between us and God, is there any controversy? Is there anything we are withholding from God?

I do not need to mention again the various departments of life, the various items that have to be surrendered. All has to be surrendered—our members are presented as instruments of righteousness unto God. These bodies are presented unto God, yielded as a living sacrifice.

You and I will never know the fullness of the Spirit of God until first of all there has been a confession and then a consecration, a yielding to God of everything.

115

One thing more, for I do not think we've reached the end yet. I think there has to be claiming. There has to be a daily walk of faith. There has to be a moment-by-moment entering into the thing that we are talking about.

When I have confessed and made right the sin, when in yieldedness to God—perhaps brought low in tears before Him in surrender—I arise and by faith claim what He offers me, then I'll know the fullness of the divine Spirit.

Dr. F. B. Meyer used to tell a story that illustrates the power of a Spirit-filled life. Let me tell it to you:

> In the best of men there is a tendency to do certain things they ought not, but the more they are filled with the Spirit, the more it is true of them that they are kept from doing what otherwise they would. When I was a boy I used to go to the Polytechnic in London, where my favourite diversion was a diving-bell, which had seats around the rim, and which at a given time was filled with people and lowered into the tank. We used to go down deeper, deeper into the water; but not a drop came into that diving-bell, though it had no bottom and the water was quite within reach, because the bell was so full of air that, though the water lusted against the air, the air lusted against

the water because the air was being pumped in all the time from the top, and the water could not do what it otherwise would do. If you are full of the Holy Ghost, the flesh life is underneath you, and though it would surge up, it is kept out.

11

A FINAL WORD

THERE ARE TWO NEW TESTAMENT words translated *perfect* which have to do with the holiness of the believer. One word (occurring only once) is in II Timothy 3:17 and has the idea of *fitted.* The second word has the sense of *maturity, full growth* (cf. Eph. 4:13; Phil. 3:15, etc.).

Speaking of these words, the Rev. W. Y. Fullerton said,

> The word *perfect* is a maligned word. There are two words in the Bible translated "perfect," but neither of them means *sinlessness.* The one means *equipment* and *adjustment,* and the other *full growth.* But that does not mean any sinless perfection in the flesh. That doctrine has never been taught at Keswick, and, please God, it never will be. Yet the blessing that comes to men and women, when fully adjusted to Jesus Christ, is so great and vital that it is not surprising that sometimes

people are apt to think they have reached the end of their struggle with sin. But the Word of God does not teach us, and the message of "Keswick" is not, that we are not able to sin, but that we are able not to sin. Have you caught that? It is not that we are not able to sin, but it is that we are able not to sin, if we keep on trusting the power that is placed at our disposal.

Our plea, then, is for spiritual living as over against carnal living, for discipleship as against mere profession.

So that it will be perfectly patent to all and perhaps will be helpful to some who might otherwise labor under a false impression, let me say a further word about the subject of conflicts. As Mr. Fullerton observed, the Word of God does not teach that we can reach the place where from henceforth there will never be a "struggle with sin" (so long as the aspirations for holiness are in our hearts).

Let me observe that our greatest battle is always with the flesh, the self-life. The greatest conflict is between self and God, between our own sinful way and God's will. Yes, other foes will withstand us. Satan, his minions, men and the world will hurl their darts. But what will they avail, if self is crucified? The vortex of the of Scottish ancestry. She listened to her son Ross as he unfolded to her what he had learned about the crucifixion of the old man, and the possibility of a life of triumph in Christ. His mother said little beyond a word of encouragement to him.

A couple of weeks after his return home from the conference, Ross was not making quite the progress in the practical experience which he could describe so well theoretically.

Finally his mother took him aside and very quietly, according to his testimony, inquired of him, "Ross, I understand that you believe the Bible teaches that your old man was crucified with Christ."

"Yes," responded Ross, "that is right."

"Well, then, Ross, I'd like to make inquiry as to why there are so many resurrections."

Now, beyond such a struggle as may characterize us when there is a controversy between us and the Lord, there is also the keen sense of battle against our other foes. I would remind you that even the most spiritual saint knows this battle. As a matter of fact, he probably knows it increasingly, the more closely he walks with God. It is just here that the child of God must believe God. God has made the provisions for our victory. By faith we take our stand, not for victory, but in His victory. The conflict is real, but the sense of His presence and power and provision are also real.

Does such a life mean there is nothing for the child of God to do? Of course not. We have already made plain that he is to fight the fight of faith. In courage born of confidence in the faithfulness of God, the child of God enters the fray. But is that all?

Let me quote from Bishop Handley C. G. Moule:

> Is this life really so effortless, so careless? Is it a life in which you simply get into a stream and swim with it, and let it take you on forever? Is that all? No, that is much, but it is not all. Hallowing and keeping grace is indeed a stream, and the stream is strong, and to be in it is blessed. Nevertheless there is a large place in the true life for labour and for pains. How does this come in? Surely with the recollection that we can use the trusted Christ only when we are *keeping awake*. And you do not keep awake by growing slack in your habits, in your devotions, in your thinking, in your self-examining, in your serving and loving; you do not keep awake by indolence in any of these matters. To take God's means that we may keep awake needs pains.

Charles Simeon of Cambridge . . . used to say

. . . "My friends, remember that justification comes by faith, but knowledge of your Bible comes by works." *We must labour with the means God has given us,* for keeping awake in spiritual consciousness. *We must take pains with praying* . . .

You must take pains with your Bible . . .

Then let us remember the ordinances of the Church . . .

Remember also private help. One precious help is Christian friendship, rightly used as a sacred trust for Christ . . .

Throughout these chapters much stress has been put upon surrender. It is most necessary that we understand what surrender really is. Surrender is not simply resignation. It is rather the joyful, happy yielding of all that one is and all that one has to the Lord Jesus Christ. To use biblical language, it is the presentation of the body, the members of the body, to the Lord Jesus Christ (Rom. 6:13; 12:1-2).

As to the meaning of such a surrender to the Lord, many will recall the helpfulness of a biblical illustration used by the saintly Andrew Murray. He referred to the historical incident of the relationship of Joseph to Potiphar. Granted, this is not a perfect illustration, yet it has many facets of truth that will help us to understand something of what our relationship should be to the Lord.

You will recall in Genesis 39 the story of Joseph's appointment as the overseer of Potiphar's palace. Potiphar by deliberate act made Joseph the master. Says the Word of God: "All that he had he put into his hand" (v. 4); "He made him overseer . . . over all that he had" (v. 5); "He left all that he had in Joseph's hand" (v. 6a); "He knew not aught that was with him, save the bread which he did eat" (v. 6b). Potiphar's committal was complete; he held back nothing of all his possessions.

The biblical account indicates that Jehovah blessed Potiphar's house "for Joseph's sake" (v. 5). Moreover, the blessing of God was upon Potiphar's house and field (both his private and his public life). Nor was Potiphar's surrender meant to be temporary. True, the story ends upon a different note. But at the outset it is clear that Potiphar's turning over the control of his possessions was complete, wholehearted and lasting: "*he left* all that he had in Joseph's hand" (v. 6).

Now, if we were to substitute the name of the Lord Jesus for that of Joseph, we have the striking parallel which Dr. Murray suggests. When you and I, as Potiphar, make the heavenly Joseph, our Lord Jesus, truly the Lord of our lives, when we put all that we have in His hands, then we shall be blessed of the Lord for Jesus' sake. It is not enough to make some sort of helper of the Lord Jesus; He must be Master.

Such a surrender calls for deep searching of heart. I suppose most of us quite willingly surrender a great deal of what we are and what we have to the Lord without any question. After all, we not only understand the reasonableness of the request that we should present our bodies a living sacrifice unto God, but we understand that there is blessing in doing so. However, there are those darlings in our lives, those personal and private habits or possessions, that somehow or other are so dear to us that we are unwilling to surrender them.

Dear Dr. F. B. Meyer used to speak of the one room, the one key, the one place of surrender that had to be made if he was to enter into all that God had for him. The trouble with some of us is that there has been a defective surrender. We haven't truly put the Lord Jesus Christ first. So if we are to enter into the life of victory, there must be a facing of this issue and a settling of it, a settling of it all in a crisis experience, but beyond that crisis experience, the daily, moment-by-moment yielding of ourselves to God.

Another striking and most apparent truth brought out in this book is that the complemental truth of surrender is faith. The possibility of living a victorious life depends upon our "looking unto Jesus" (Heb. 12:2). The provisions of God are sufficient, but it is only faith that will link us with the Source of supply. There is a text in Paul's epistle to the Colossians which succinctly sets forth precisely what the case is. "As therefore ye received Christ Jesus the Lord, so walk in him" (Col. 2:6). Surely the Christian knows and understands that it was by faith that he entered into salvation and that justification is by faith. This text makes very plain that sanctification demands faith as well.

If your statement is that such a means, such an instrument, is too simple, let me remind you that, though salvation is most profound and the cost of it is utterly beyond our comprehension, the way in which we entered into the salvation of God was simplicity itself. It took a childlike faith, a simple trust in the Lord Jesus. So as we received Christ Jesus the Lord, that is the way we shall also walk in Him, namely, by the exercise of the same childlike faith, the same simple trust.

In conclusion, let me speak from my heart in a very personal way. It is my deep conviction that true Christian living is a miracle. The Christian life, so far as our experience on earth is concerned, will be consummated in the miraculous translation of the child of God into the presence of the Lord, whether it is without the body in death or whether it is in the transformed body at the coming of the Lord Jesus Christ. May I affirm that Christian living in the present also calls for nothing less than the supernatural working of our great God. We cannot live the Christian life ourselves. The Lord of glory, the Lord Jesus Christ, the blessed and only Son of the living God, is the only One who can enable us to live as we should.

We have seen some of God's provisions for us to live victoriously. May God help us to enter into them. May I say for my part, that without any claim to sinlessness, indeed, without any claim to spirituality at all, I can as a follower of the Lord Jesus Christ say with deep conviction that the possibility of victorious Christian living is very real. God has given us Himself. But remember, the instruments which we must exercise (only with God's enablings, of course) are a committed will, which involves the complete surrender of all that we are and have to Him, and a daily and moment-by-moment walk in faith, trusting Him to perform the miracle.

battle is the personal element. When we will to do His will, we have taken the first step toward the realization of the victory He has already won for us.

Is the place of your conflict your controversy with the will of God? Then no wonder there is conflict; how could there help but be? "Wretched man that I am! Who shall deliver me out of the body of this death?" (Rom. 7:24). That utterance may well be your cry; but that cry has an answer: "I thank God through Jesus Christ our Lord" (v. 25).

End this conflict by surrender!

But that is not to say that all sense of struggle will be over. The self-life never dies easily. Put to death today, it has a way of reviving tomorrow. Remember that a crisis surrender must be followed by daily yielding.

I well recall an illustration growing out of an early acquaintance with the teaching of Scripture concerning victorious living. A friend of mine in company with several of us attended a conference on the victorious life. My friend was greatly helped and blessed. He rejoiced greatly in the message of the Word of God as it was unfolded to him. On his return home he proceeded to tell his mother what happened. I should relate to you that his mother was a real Christian